PHILLIS WHEATLEY IN THE BLACK AMERICAN BEGINNINGS

(Broadside Critics Series Number 5.

James A. Emanuel, General Editor)

ABOUT THE SERIES COVER

The cord represents literary creativity which has a strong tradition among African peoples. The tradition is found in the great store of oral history, in the contextual writing which forms designs seen on buildings, calabashes and other useful objects. It is implicit in many figurative designs and sculpture.

Several times in the history of the people, the cord has been severed abruptly—but continues again in a rich store of literary works represented here in the Broadside Critics Series.

—Cledie Taylor

PHILLIS WHEATLEY IN THE BLACK AMERICAN BEGINNINGS

by

William H. Robinson

bp

BROADSIDE PRESS
12651 Old Mill Place Detroit, Michigan 48238

First Edition
First Printing

ISBN: 0-910296-18-9 cloth $6.00
ISBN: 0-910296-27-8 paper $3.50

Manufactured in the U.S.A.

Acknowledgments

I wish to thank the following authors, libraries and publishers for their kind permissions to reprint selections from their works:

The Massachusetts Historical Society for "A Poem on the Death of Charles Eliot, aged 12 months"; "An address to the Atheist, by P. Wheatley at the age of 14 years—1767"; "Atheism—Boston, July, 1769"; and "An address to the Deist—1767."

Sarah Dunlap Jackson for "Letters of Phillis Wheatley and Susanna Wheatley," *Journal of Negro History,* LVII No. 2 (April, 1972). Copyright, 1972, by The Association for the Study of Negro Life and History, Inc.

Lorenzo J. Greene for *The Negro in Colonial New England: 1620-1776* (New York: Columbia University Press, 1942) Copyright, 1942, by Columbia University Press.

Broadside Press, Detroit, Michigan, for "Nikki Rosa" from *Black Judgement,* Copyright © 1968, by Nikki Giovanni.

The Historical Society of Pennsylvania for excerpts from "An Addrass (sic) to the Blacks in Philadelphia 9th month 1787," as edited by Melvin H. Buxbaum, "Cyrus Bustill Addresses the Black in Philadelphia," *William and Mary Quarterly,* Third Series, XXIX (January, 1972).

Julian D. Mason, *The Poems of Phillis Wheatley* (Chapel Hill Univ. of North Carolina Press, 1966). Copyright 1966, by The University of North Carolina Press.

Table of Contents

Preface

The following few pages mean to suggest that a new reading of Phillis Wheatley's poetry is in order, especially when consideration is given to the realities—racial, social, religious, literary—of her primitive Colonial times. It will be seen that Phillis more than held her own as a poet and as an aware Black woman; that she has long since earned a secure place in the development of Black American literature in ways not hitherto recorded.

I wish to thank friends, colleagues, students, but especially librarians at Massachusetts Historical Society and at the John Carter Brown and Rockefeller Libraries of Brown University. I want also to thank the following authors and publishers for kind permissions to reprint from their works: Nikki Giovanni, for an excerpt from "Nikki Rosa"; Dr. Lorenzo J. Greene, for excerpts from *The Negro in Colonial New England: 1620-1776;* Sara Dunlap Jackson, for excerpts from "Letters of Phillis Wheatley and Susanna Wheatley" in *Journal of Negro History;* Professor Julian D. Mason, Jr., for excerpts from *The Poems of Phillis Wheatley.* As always, and gratefully, do I want to thank my wife, Doris Carol.

Phillis Wheatley
In the Black American Beginnings

Easily among the most renowned—and therefore the most variously interpreted—Afro-American poets, Phillis Wheatley, from the time of her teens in the 1760's, when she was astonishing literary America by publishing her poetry as broadsides and in leading Boston and Philadelphia magazines, to this day, has sustained a lively, controversial reputation. Commentary has ranged from Black and white critical acclaim, sometimes close to rhapsodic awe, to Black and white critical denigration, sometimes close to rank polemicizing. From the 18th century to well into the 20th, the poet has had her ever increasing arrays of adversaries and advocates, each group finding only what it wished to see in this precocious New England slave poet, neither group viewing *all* of her writing or considering the pressures of her times. As a consequence, if a fair appraisal of this woman is to be reached, the fullest possible examination of her life and work is necessary. But there is not, in these few pages, space enough either to cite adequately these still growing trans opinionated works or to use all the extant relevant data on her. As was pointed out almost forty years ago by the first important Black critic of the poet's work, "The bibliography of the works of Phillis Wheatley is now a study in itself."[1] Selections of traditional criticism of her work will be included here, but the emphasis will be on samplings reflecting *all* of her poetry and prose, with consideration of the realities of her colonial times, in an attempt to show that, once comprehensively read, she emerges as someone different from what tradition contends.

Her Life

Biographical sketches and "memoirs," various, and often contradictory, present different Phillis Wheatleys. Charlotte Ruth Wright, who has contributed her own memoir, wrote in 1930, "Exactly fifty-three times have the poems of Phillis Wheatley been printed either in book form or folio."[2] Many of these reprintings contain a "sketch" of the life of the poet.

Reading many of these sketches, however, soon makes it clear that, by acknowledgment or not, they are traceable back to the memoir written by Margaretta Matilda Odell for the 1834 reprinting of the 1773 volume of collected poems. This memoir is the most valuable because, although written fifty years after the poet's death, the author was "a collateral descendant of Mrs. Wheatley, and has been familiar with the name and fame of Phillis from her childhood."[3] Moreover, Miss Odell derived her facts from "grand-nieces of Phillis' benefactress, who are still living,"[4] facts which were later corroborated. Also seminal in its help is another sketch, published by Dr. Nathaniel B. Shurtleff in the December 21, 1863, issue of the Boston *Daily Advertiser*. It contains "a few facts relating to this remarkable woman, which are not generally known, and some of which have escaped her biographers."[5] Later research has corrected its slight mistakes. In the August 3, 1761, issue of the Boston *Evening Post,* and for a number of weeks thereafter, appeared the following advertisement:

To Be Sold

A parcel of likely Negroes, imported from Africa, cheap for cash, or short Credit; Enquire of John Avery, at his House next Door to the White-Horse, or at a Store adjoining to said Avery's Distill-House, at the South End, near the South Market; Also, if any Persons have any Negro Men, strong and hearty, tho' not of

> the best moral character, which are proper Subjects for Transportation, may have an Exchange for *small Negroes.* (Italics mine)

Among these "small Negroes" was, very likely, the child who would become known as Phillis Wheatley, for, as one man remembered, years later:

> Aunt Wheatley was in want of a domestic. She went aboard to purchase. In looking through the ship's company of living freight, her attention was drawn to that of a slender, frail female child, which at once enlisted her sympathies. Owing to the frailty of the child, she procured her for a trifle, as the captain had fears of her dropping off his hands, without emolument, by death.[6]

When she was bought "for a trifle," Phillis was reckoned to be "about seven years old . . . from the circumstance of shedding her front teeth. She soon gave indications of uncommon intelligence, and was frequently seen endeavoring to make letters upon the wall with a piece of chalk or charcoal."[7] Much impressed, Mrs. Wheatley made special provisions for the development of Phillis. Instead of being kept busy at the usual menial domestic labors, Phillis was befriended by the entire family and tutored by Mary Wheatley, a daughter. Learning to read and write, she became quickly proficient in "astronomy, ancient and modern geography, and ancient history," English and Latin literature, and (the Wheatleys being devout) the Bible," the most difficult parts of which she could read within sixteen months."[8] She "soon attracted the attention of the literati of the day, many of whom furnished her with books. . . . She was frequently visited by clergymen, and other individuals of high standing in society."[9] Phillis was supplied with paper and pencil by her bedside to accommodate any night-time inspiration for her verse writing.

However indulged she was in the Wheatley household, Phillis was very much aware of colonial white American racism, for

> whenever she was invited to the households of individuals of wealth and distinction (which frequently happened) she always

declined the seat offered her at their board, and, requesting that a side-table might be laid for her, dined modestly apart from the rest of the company.[10]

On the other hand, there is the anecdote recalling her once being invited to dine with a Colonel and Mrs. Fitch, whose three status-conscious daughters objected on the grounds of race. Over their objections, Mrs. Fitch insisted. Phillis, seated with the family, proceeded to regale the three daughters with well-narrated stories. "As she went on with her stories, they forgot her color and that she had been a slave; they felt no prejudice against her because she was black, and they felt ashamed that they had ever made objections to her having a seat at their table."[11]

Even when Phillis did perform various household chores, it was with uncommon attention to other things going on, as is evident from the descriptive headnote of her very first published poem, appearing in the Newport (Rhode Island) *Mercury,* December 21, 1767:

> To the Printer./Please to insert the following Lines, composed by a/Negro girl/(belonging to one Mr. Wheatley of Boston) on the following/Occasion, viz. Messrs. Hussey and Coffin, as undermentioned, be-/longing to Nantucket, being bound from thence to Boston, nar/rowly escaped being cast away on Cape Cod, in one of the late/Storms; upon their Arrival, being at Mr. Wheatley's and while/at Dinner, told of their narrow escape, this Negro girl at/the same Time 'tending Table, heard the Relations, from which she composed the following Verses.

On Messrs. Hussey and Coffin.

Did Fear and Danger so perplex your Mind,
As made you fearful of the whistling Wind?
Was it not Boreas knit his angry Brows
Against you? or did consideration bow?
To lend you Aid, did not his Winds combine?
To stop your passage with a churlish Line,
Did haughty Eolus with Contempt look down
With aspect windy, and a study'd Frown?
Regard them not:—The Great Supreme, the Wise
Intends for something hidden from our Eyes.
Suppose the groundless Gulph had snatch'd away

Hussey and Coffin to the raging Sea;
Where wou'd they go? where wou'd be their Abode?
With the supreme and independent God,
Or made their Beds down in the Shades below,
Where neither Pleasure nor Content can stow.
To heaven their Souls with eager Raptures soar,
Enjoy the Bliss of him they wou'd adore.
Had the soft gliding Streams of Grace been near,
Some favourite Hope their fainting Hearts to cheer,
Doubtless the Fear of Danger far had fled:
No more repeated Victory crown their Heads.
Had I the Tongue of a Seraphim, how would I exalt thy
Praise: thy Name as incense to the Heavens should fly,
and the/Remembrance of thy Goodness to the shoreless
Ocean of Beati-/tude!—Then should the earth glow
with seraphick Ardour./
Blest Soul, which sees the Day while Light doth shine,
To guide his steps to trace the Mark divine.

Phillis Wheatley[12]

This verse is remarkable for several reasons, including its felt fervor, its imagistic ambition, and, the italicized prose lines notwithstanding, its relative maturity. Already discernible is her profound spirituality, a sense that she would manifest in her life, poems and letters throughout her years. Phillis continued her poetry writing until 1770, when she composed "On the Death of the Rev. Mr. George Whitefield, 1770." Published in at least ten editions in Boston, Newport, Philadelphia, and in 1771, in London, this poem extended and solidly established her international reputation. George Whitefield (1714-1770) was an extremely popular English-born evangelist who preached throughout the American colonies, even converting and befriending American Blacks, e.g., John Marrant (about whom more later). Moreover, Whitefield was a beloved chaplain to the celebrated Countess of Huntingdon (Selina Hastings, 1707-1791), wealthy, eccentric religionist promoter of early English Methodism. Phillis' elegy on Whitefield, accompanied by a covering letter, went far to recommend her into the considerable graces of the Countess:

To the R.t. Hon'ble the Countess of Huntingdom

Most noble Lady

The Occasion of my addressing your Ladiship will, I hope, apologize for this my boldness in doing it. It is to enclose a few lines on the decease of your worthy chaplain, the Rev Mr. Whitefield, in the loss of whom I sincerely sympathize with your Ladiship: but your great loss which is his Greater gain, will, I hope, meet with infinite reparation, in the presence of God, the Divine Benefactor whose image you bear by filial imitation.

The Tongues of the Learned are insufficient, much less the pen of an untutor'd African, to paint in lively character, the excellencies of this citizen of Zion! I beg an interest in your Ladiship's Prayer and am,

With great humility
Your Ladiship's most obedient
Humble servant
Phillis Wheatley

Boston Oct. 25th 1770[13]

Impressively as her career was going, however, Phillis was to know some setbacks. January 31, 1771, her long-time devoted tutor, Mary Wheatley, left the Wheatley household to become the wife of the Reverend John Lothrop, pastor of the Second Church in Boston. This loss was somewhat offset later when, on August 18, 1771, "Phillis, the servant of Mr. Wheatley," was baptized and received as a communicant in the famous Old South Meeting house by the celebrated Reverend Dr. Samuel Cooper.[14] It must be understood that, popular and gifted as she was, Phillis was obliged to sit, with other Blacks, in "the reserved section" of the Christian church.

As may be gathered from the newspaper description of her as a frail, young, kidnapped African, newly landed in Boston, and as is confirmed repeatedly in several of her later letters to a fellow female African servant, Arbour (sometimes spelled "Obur") Tanner, living in Newport, Rhode Island, Phillis was always fragile, small and delicate, and asthmatic, her condition annually aggravated by bone-cold New England winters. Indeed, she became so ill that, fearing for her life, the Wheatley doctors prescribed a trip to London for recuperation. Mrs. Susanna Wheatley, not well herself, made arrangements for the trip, which also involved promotion for the long-awaited publication of Phillis' collected poems in a single volume. Mrs. Wheatley wrote, April 30, 1773, to the Countess of Huntingdon, thanking her for permitting the poet to dedicate the proposed volume to her, and for asking for the striking of Phillis' engraving as frontispiece to the volume. The maternalistic Mrs. Wheatley also mentioned these provisions for her twenty-year-old protègée:

> I tell Phillis to act wholly under the direction of your Ladiship. I did not think it worth while nor did the time permit it to fit her out with cloaths: but I have given her money to Buy what you think most proper for her. I like she should be dress'd plain. Must beg the favor of your Ladiship to advise my son to some Christian Home for Phillis to board at.[15]

Escorted by Nathaniel Wheatley, the son going to England to expand his father's merchant business, and aboard Mr. Wheatley's ship *London,* Phillis sailed for London in May, 1773. Abroad, she was reportedly feted by ranking personalities and clergymen as a Black prodigy. The ubiquitous Benjamin Franklin wrote, "I went to see the black poetess, and offered her any service I could do for her."[16] She was given many valuable gifts, especially books, which included a 1770 Glasgow folio edition of *Paradise Lost,* presented by Brooks Watson, Lord Mayor of London, and a copy of Tobias Smollett's 1770 translation of *Don Quixote.* The Countess of Huntingdon was, unfortunately, in Wales throughout Phillis' brief stay in London. Nevertheless, the poet completed plans for her *Poems on Various Subjects, Religious and Moral,* "first published in London, from the original manuscript, by Arch Bell, Aldgate, 1773." This was the first volume of poetry published by an American Black writer. Having likely read all of these poems in earlier versions, Mrs. Wheatley was concerned more with the accuracy of the engraving of Phillis:

> Phillis was well received in England, was presented to . . . many . . . individuals of distinction. . . . During her stay, her poems were given to the world, dedicated to the Countess of Huntingdon, and embellished with an engraving which is said

to have been a striking representation of the original. It is supposed that one of these impressions was forwarded to her mistrees (in Boston) as soon as they were struck off; for a grandniece of Mrs. Wheatley informs us that, during the absence of Phillis, she one day called upon her relative, who immediately directed her attention to a picture over the fireplace, exclaiming—"See! look at my Phillis, does she not seem as though she would speak to me!"[17]

Before she could see all of the English celebrities she wished to see, including King George III, she was obliged to return to Boston, for Mrs. Wheatley was seriously ill. In a letter from London, July 17, 1773, Phillis explained to the Countess in Wales: ". . . Am sorry to acquaint your Ladiship that the Ship is certainly to sail next Thursday (on) which I must return to America. I long to see my Friend there. . . ."[18]

Upon her return to America in July, Phillis' good fortunes declined. Writing to her Black friend, Obour Tanner, October 30, 1773, Phillis confided, "My mistress has been sick above 14 weeks, & confined to her bed the whole time, but is I hope somewhat better now."[19] But Mrs. Wheatley died March 3, 1774. March 21, Phillis confessed her grief to her friend Obour Tanner:

DEAR OBOUR,— . . . I have lately met with a great trial in the death of my mistress; let us imagine the loss of a parent, sister, or brother, the tenderness of all these were united in her. I was a poor little outcast & a stranger when she took me in: not only into her house, but I presently became a sharer in her most tender affections. I was treated by her more like a child than her servant; no opportunity was left unimproved of giving me the best of advice; but in terms how tender! how engaging! This I hope ever to keep in remembrance. Her examplary life was a greater monitor than all her precepts and instruction. . . .[20]

March 12, 1778, her master, John Wheatley, died, and that September Mary Wheatley (Lothrop) died. For the very first time in her sheltered life, Phillis was obliged to shift for herself, contending with the chaos of revolutionary fervor and as a poet and a seamstress, struggling to make a living. After Mr. Wheatley died, she lived briefly with a Wheatley relative in Boston, and then took an apartment by herself. Phillis understood very well that these were not the most congenial times for her most valuable commodity, poetry. She seems to have then yielded to the blandishments of one of what may have been several Black wooers, for it is recorded that "John Peters married Phillis Wheatley, *free Negroes,* April 1, 1778, Boston [italics mine]."[21] Phillis had known John Peters since at least 1773, when, October 30, she mentioned him in a postscript to a letter to Miss Tanner: "The young man by whom this is handed you seems to me to be a very clever man, knows you very well, & is very complaisant and agreeable."[22]

But about him there is much contradictory evidence, most of it disparaging (and most of it from white sources). One source contends that he was

> a respectable colored man of Boston. . . . He kept a grocery in Court-Street, and was a man of very handsome person and manners; wore a wig, carried a cane, and quite acted out "the gentleman." . . . he proved utterly unworthy of the distinguished woman who honored him by her alliance. He was unsuccessful in business, and failed soon after their marriage; and is said to have been both too proud and too indolent to apply himself to any occupation below his fancied dignity.[23]

Another writer feels that "Peters not only bore a good character, but was in every way a remarkable specimen of his race, being a fluent writer, a ready speaker and an intelligent man."[24] There are other versions of the man. Along with countless others, Phillis and John Peters fled the British seige of Boston, these two going to Wilmington, Massachusetts, where Phillis apparently gave birth to one or more children. She mothered three, but their origins are not known exactly. They were all born in feeble health. In Wilmington, an obscure village, Phillis' downright poverty was compounded severely. Since colonial white America was not yet ready for a self-confident Black John Peters, Phillis had a hard time supporting her children:

> After the evacuation of Boston by the British, Phillis returned

thither. A Niece of Mrs. Wheatley, whose son had been slain in battle, received her beneath her own roof. This lady was a widow, and not wealthy. She kept a small day school to increase her narrow income. Her mansion had been much injured by the enemy, but it afforded a shelter to herself and her daughter, and they ministered to Phillis and her three suffering children, for six weeks. At the end of that period, Peters came for his wife, and, having provided an apartment, took her thither with her little family.[25]

Strained at best, the marriage was lamented by most observers—except Shirley Graham DuBois in her freely romanticized children's book, *The Life of Phillis Wheatley* (1949). Indeed the union was regretted internationally. Wrote Abbé Grègoire, a zealous French Negrophile:

> La sensible Phillis, qui avoit été gâté,élevée . . . en enfant n'entendoit rien â gouverner un ménage, et son mari vouloit qu'elle s'en occupât; il commença par des reproches auxquels succédèrent de mauvais traitements dont la continuité affligea tellement son épouse, qu'elle périt de chagrin.[26]
>
> (The sensitive Phillis, who had been reared almost as a spoiled child, had little or no sense or need of how to manage a household, and her husband wanted her to do just that; he made his wishes known at first by reproaches and followed these with downright bad treatment, the continuation of which so afflicted his wife that she grieved herself to death.)

Although a man of law and a member of the Massachusetts Historical Society remembered seeing Peters in the Boston courts (perhaps as a free lance advocate for hapless Blacks), Obour Tanner, whom he never offered marriage, snapped, "Poor Phillis let herself down by marrying; yes ma'am."[27] While still other reports of the marriage vary, it was clearly often embarrassing, at least, for Phillis. After Peters placed her in the apartment, in a Negro boarding house in a run-down section of Boston, Phillis was shortly obliged to work to earn her subsistence.

A relative of Mrs. Wheatley finally discovered the poet's illness and sought her out.

> She was also visited by several other members of that family.

They found her in a situation of extreme misery. Two of her children were dead, and the third was sick unto death. She was herself suffering for want of attention, for many comforts, and that greatest of all comforts in sickness—cleanliness. She was reduced to a condition too loathsome to describe. If a charitable individual, moved at the sight of so much distress, sent a load of wood, her husband *was too much of a gentleman* to prepare it for her use. . . . In a filthy apartment, in an obscure part of the metropolis, lay dying the mother, and the wasting child. The woman who had stood honored and respected in the presence of the wise and good of that country which was hers by adoption, or rather compulsion, who had graced the ancient halls of Old England, and rolled about in the splendid equippages of the proud nobles of Britain, was numbering the last hours of life in a state of the most abject misery, surrounded by all the emblems of a squalid poverty! . . .[28]

With such a grim report of Phillis' last years in mind, many observers are amazed that, withal, Mrs. John Peters still wrote and published poetry. Indeed, she even collected enough poems and letters to advertise in the Boston *Evening Post and General Advertiser* for several week in 1779, *"Dedicated to the Right Hon. Benjamin Franklin, Esq: One of the Ambassadors of the United States at the Court of France,"* the proposed volume was to have included 33 poems and 13 letters. The "Conditions" state that it

will be printed on good paper and a neat Type; and will contain about 300 pages in Octavo.

The price to Subscribers will be *Twelve Pounds,* neatly Bound & Lettered, and *Nine Pounds* sew'd in blue paper, one Half to be paid on Subscribing, the other Half on delivery of the Books.

The Work will be put to the Press as soon as a sufficient Number of Encouragers offer.[29]

This proposed second volume never was published, due largely to postwar inflation and investment trends. Nevertheless, Phillis went on writing individual poems. Celebrating the end of the Revolutionary War, "Liberty and Peace," by "Phillis Peters," appeared in 1784; "An Elegy,/ Sacred to the Memory of that/Great Divine,/The Reverend and Learned /Dr. Samuel Cooper,/. . . ," by

"Phillis Peters," appeared January 2, 1784; and, selected from the manuscript of her proposed second volume, "written by PHILLIS PETERS, formerly PHILLIS WHEATLEY," another poem, "To Mr. and Mrs.——, on the Death of Their Infant Son," was published September, 1784, just three months before she was to die. Two letters written by Phillis after she was married are important here. One, dated Boston May 29th '78, she signs as "Phillis Wheatley," but she refers to her new address and husband: "Direct your letters under cover to Mr. John Peters in Queen Street." The other, dated Boston May 10, 1779, she signs as "Phillis Peters." The point of these references to Phillis' use of her married name, despite the reported wretchedness of her last days, is to question the objectivity in her biographer's denigrating John Peters as the husband in passages like the following:

> . . . we never hear Phillis named, or alluded to, by any other appellation than that of "Phillis Wheatley"— a name which she sustained with dignity and honor. . . .[30]

Also, given her apparent subjectivity, her biographer, a white woman, was viewing Peters from a white perspective. To her, Peters, who seems to have been beholden to no one, including whites, might have appeared arrogant, unseemly and objectionable as otherwise described. But, from a Black perspective, his marriage might not have been drastically broken. Nikki Giovanni expresses the point best:

> and I really hope no white person ever has cause
> to write about me
> because they never understand
> Black love is Black wealth and they'll
> probably talk about my hard childhood
> and never understand that
> all the while I was quite happy[31]

Nevertheless, Phillis' last days and her death were remembered pathetically by some:

> Little more remains to be told . . . the friends of Phillis, who

> had visited her in her sickness, knew not of her death. Peters did not see fit to acquaint them with the event, or to notify them of her interment. A grand-niece of Phillis' benefactress, passing up Court-Street, met the funeral of an adult and a child: a bystander informed her they were bearing Phillis Wheatley to that silent mansion. . . .[32]

On December 5, 1784, aged thirty-one, Phillis Wheatley Peters died in Boston, a famous poet, a Black woman, wife and mother. Several area newspapers published her obituary, but is is not yet known exactly where Phillis and the last of her children were buried.

Peters then, seems to have been a proud Black man too ambitious for the racist realities of colonial times. Not only was he in and out of jail while Phillis was alive, but Phillis' *Paradise Lost,* still in Harvard University, contains the following inscription (written by a white admirer of Phillis):

> This book was given by Brook Watson formerly Lord Mayor of London to Phillis Wheatley & after her death was sold in payment of her husband's debts. It is now presented to the Library of Harvard University at Cambridge, by Dudley L. Pickman of Salem. March, 1824.

Finally, after Phillis' death, Peters went to the daughter of the woman who, after the evacuation of Boston, had taken Phillis and her children in for six weeks, and demanded the manuscript of the proposed second volume of poems and letters. The manuscript, "as the property of his deceased wife was of course yielded to his importunity. Some years after, he went to the South, and we have not been able to ascertain what eventually became of the manuscripts."[33]

Her Poetry

The aforementioned polarity among critics of Phillis Wheatley's poetry has been predictable in a racist America, where "from the very first, Negro literature was chained to the issue of racial equality."[34] Very rarely was Phillis' poetry viewed for its intrinsic literary worth. Almost always her work was valued in terms of how it could be contorted into cultural anthropology written in iambic pentameter and rimed couplets. Her many white advocates among her acquaintances and contemporaries included distinguished men and women. Prefacing her celebrated 1773 volume, in attestation of the slave poet's authenticity, are the names of eighteen of "the most respectable Characters in Boston," including His Excellency Thomas Hutchinson, Governor of Massachussetts, 1771-1774; the Honorable Andrew Oliver, Lieutenant-Governor; John Hancock of Boston; the Honorable James Bowdoin; the Reverend Matthew Byles, Tory poet. Many of these, it should be remembered, were slavetraders and slaveholders.[35] Not on this list, but equally prominent, was another advocate of Phillis' poetic abilities, Dr. Benjamin Rush of Philadelphia, signer of the Declaration of Independence, member of the Continental Congress, humanitarian, who wrote in 1774:

> There is now in the town of Boston a free Negro Girl, about eighteen years of age, who has been but nine years in the country, whose singular genius and accomplishments are such as not only do honour to her sex, but to human nature. Several of her poems have been printed, and read with pleasure by the public.[36]

The Marquis de Barbe-Marbois, Secretary to the French Legation during the Revolutionary War, thought Phillis was

> one of the strangest creatures in the country and perhaps in the world. . . . Phyllis [sic] is a negress, born in Africa. . . . She learned English with unusual ease, eagerly read and reread the Bible . . . became steeped in the poetic image of which it is full, and at the age of seventeen published a number of poems in which there is imagination, poetry, and zeal, though no correctness nor order nor interest. I read them with some surprise. They are printed, and in the front of the book there are certificates of authenticity which leave no doubt that she is its author.[37]

In a letter to Baron Constant de Bebecq, the informed

Voltaire offered his views on Phillis the Black poet: "Fontenelle avait tort de dire qu'il n' y aurait jamais de poètes chez les Nègres: il y at actuellement une Négresse qui fait de très-bons vers anglais.[38] (Fontenelle was wrong to say that there would never be a Negro poet; there is actually a Negro woman who writes very good English verse.) And the Massachusetts Historical Society is responsible for the continuing publication of much of her work, including first publication of her letters to Obour (Arbour) Tanner, and helpful secondary information.

To be sure, persons as eminent as Phillis always attract as many adversaries as advocates. Quite early in the history of Phillis' denigrators was the well-known, bigoted remark of Thomas Jefferson, who wrote, "Religion, indeed, has produced a Phyllis [sic] Wheatley; but it could not produce a poet. The compositions published under her name are below the dignity of criticism." Reactions to Jefferson were immediate and they quickly proliferated. Indeed, much of the early Wheatley criticism is essentially rebuttal of Jeffersonian disdain. Perhaps less well known is the carping criticism of other early white observers. One Bernard Romans, "a capable but unorthodox natural philosopher," cajoled Benjamin Rush and others for extolling Phillis as

> a single example of a negro girl writing a few silly poems to prove that the blacks are not deficient to us in understanding . . . . against the Phillis of Boston (who is the Phoenix of her race) I could bring at least twenty well known instances of the contrary effect of education on this sable generation.[39]

Another denigrator put together a wrenched ballad-stanza satire in broadside form and published it in New York in 1828. The sorry piece features a crude woodcut of three burly Black women beating brooms against several oversized, armed white men and apparently relates to some actual, specific racial confrontation. Using misspelled words to approximate the writer's stereotyped notion of Blacks' speech, the satire is entitled "Dreadful Riot on Negro

Hill,/O Read with detention de Melancholy Tale, and he sends you yelling to your bed!" Heading the 29 stanzas is a notation: "Copy of a letter from Phillis, to her sister in the cuntry, describing the Riot on Negro Hill. Bosson, Ulie, 27th, 180028 [i.e., Boston, July 27, 1828]":

> Dear Sisser—I hab sad tidin' to enform you. O a few night since I taught lass day surely come. A great number of white truckerman get angry/wid count I spose so many bad girl who lib here, and treten to molish all de brack peoples housen! I don't know dat I can gib you more sublime description of/de dreadful spot of work, den in de language of Massa Pope and Milton.[40]

The work concludes with an N.B. "By de great destruction of my furniture you will perceive my house was pretty genteel furnish—common furniture will do in de country, but in Bosson or Providence if a body wish to be reckon anything dey muss conform to fashion ob de place."[41]

Recently, a team of white editors of Black literature contended that a nineteenth century critic's approval of Phillis

> stems primarily from the fact that this Negro poetess so well fits the Uncle Tom syndrome, which the writer obviously takes to be the Negro norm. She is pious, graceful and civil ("civility is natural to them"). He cites with approval her delicacy in not sitting at the same table with whites even when invited to do so, "lest her color offend them," and points out that Phillis didn't marry until all her white friends had either died or scattered—and this marriage, to a Negro, turned out to be unfortunate. . . .[42]

There are many other white critics who, like the examples above, have more to say about Phillis' race than they do about her work.

More important is Phillis' poetic reputation as it has fared among American Black readers. As with white observers, Black critics are also often divided into those damning her and those praising her, both assuming one stance or another because of whatever Black militant assertiveness they see or do not see in her poetry. Blacks began to write criticism of Phillis more recently than whites: only after she was dead did they refer to her in their speeches and comments. Bold, outspoken Martin R. Delany, among the earlier Blacks who wrote down their feelings concerning Phillis, commented with characteristic vigor:

> In the year 1773, though held in servitude, and without the advantages or privileges of the schools of the day, accomplishing herself by her own perseverance, Phillis Wheatley appeared in the arena, the brilliancy of whose genius, as a poetess, delighted Europe and astonished America, and by a special act of the British Parliament, 1773, her productions were published for the Crown. . . . though young [she] was a person of no ordinary mind, no common attainments; but at the time, one of the brightest ornaments among the American literati. She was also well versed in Latin, in which language she composed several pieces.[43]

More restrained (and more accurate), Charlotte Forten, Philadelphia-born, Salem, Massachussetts-educated Black woman, recorded in her diary for July 28, 1854:

> This evening read Poems of Phillis Wheatley [sic] an African slave who lived in Boston at the time of the Revolution. She was a wonderfully gifted woman and many of her poems are very beautiful. Her character and genius afford a striking proof of the falseness of the assertion made by some that hers is an inferior race. . . .[44]

Other nineteenth century Blacks made similar remarks, but it was not until 1918, with the publication of Benjamin Brawley's *The Negro in Literature and Art,* that Phillis received her first extended and balanced critical evaluation by a competent Black critic. Also, in his *Early Negro American Writers* (1935), Brawley was the first anthologist to include generous and representative samplings of her work.

Phillis' lesser Black critics are in supply enough also, but especially harsh are some modern Black writers. Imamu Baraka writes:

> The mediocrity of what has been called "Negro Literature" is

> one of the most loosely held secrets of American culture. From Phyllis [sic] Wheatley to Charles Chesnutt, to the present generation of American Negro writers, the only recognizable accretion readily attributable to the black producer of a formal literature in this country, with a few notable exceptions, has been of an almost agonizing mediocrity. . . . Phyllis [sic] Wheatley and her pleasant imitations of 18th century English poetry are far and, finally, ludicrous departures from the huge black voices that splintered southern nights with their *hollers, chants, arwhoolies,* and *ballits.*[45]

Another modern Black critic finds that

> Like Freneau, she borrowed extensively from the poetical forms of the English neoclassicists. However, unlike Freneau, she failed to use these forms to call a new nation into being. *Oblivious to the lot of her fellow blacks,* she sang not of a separate nation, but of a Christian Eden. She wrote, as Richard Wright so aptly put it "as a Negro reacting, not as a Negro."[46] (italics mine)

A Black cultural historian has recently written:

> The more profound one's doubt [i.e., about one's self] the more his work is likely to be recognizable echoes of reflections of past greats. This explains why Phyllis [sic] Wheatley's voice was that of a feeble Alexander Pope rather than that of an African prince.[47]

Most condemnatory are some modern Blacks who dismiss Phillis out of hand as "an early Boston Aunt Jemina," "a colonial handkerchief head," "utterly irrelevant to the identification and liberation of the Black man." These readers express the sentiments of an early white critic, Vernon Loggins, who felt that

> Her intimate personal interests were ignored. She composed verses on the deaths of those who meant little to her, but, so far as we know, she remained silent after the deaths of Mrs. Wheatley and Mrs. Lathrop and her own children. She dwelt at length on the common notions of the day regarding liberty, but she neglected almost entirely her own state of slavery and the miserable oppression of thousands of her race.[48]

There is some truth in what Loggins contends, but only

some truth. It will here be shown that Miss Phillis Wheatley was much more personal than is commonly noted; that she composed verses *only* for people who meant much to to her in a practical way; that Mrs. Phillis Wheatley Peters was trying to do her level best to help support a growing family headed by a proud, Black inflexible man during a time of almost total community upheaval: there was a war going on. There is, of course, much truth, as always, in what Imamu Baraka says, but even greater truths must be considered. Reared and "educated" in Boston under genteel conditions, and never having even visited the South, how can she justly be charged with being a "ludicrous departure from the huge black *hollers, chants, arwhoolies,* and *ballits*" which she never heard? While she certainly knew, every day of her Black life, Boston and Massachusetts slavery, and Northern racial prejudice, she knew very little about the contemporary Black South that would historically become the womb for the birth of the archetypical Afro-American. It does not follow that Phillis *had* to versify *"hollers, chants, arwhoolies, and ballits"* to make her points. Any number of great Black literary figures, born and reared in and out of the South, have made themselves heard without using these forms. There is truth, too, in what Gayle says, but, again, only some truth. If by saying "she failed to use these forms to call a new nation into being" he means that she did not protest the evils of slavery and therefore did not help create a new and just America, he reckons without considering the gross racism of her times. If that charge means, more literally, that she felt no sense of responsibility for a nationalistic uplift of her fellow Blacks, he reckons without a full appreciation of all her writings. That she was "oblivious to the lot of her fellow blacks" is demonstrably dubious, as will be shown. The charge that, suffering identity crisis, Phillis' voice was "that of a feeble Alexander Pope rather than that of an African singer" has been already considered.

Her own contemporaries, including the Wheatley family, pressed her to recall her African background. But, having been stolen at age seven or eight and transported on a slave ship thousands of miles, Phillis did not "seem to have preserved any remembrances of the place of her navitity, or of her parents, excepting the simple circumstance that her mother poured out water before the sun at his rising—in reference, no doubt, to an ancient African custom."[49] Further, to indict Phillis for being imitative might be a modern luxury; her practice most assuredly in her time called for commendation. Neo-classical style, proudly imitative, spurned poetic originality in the Romantic sense, whether in the form of new "metaphysical conceits" or "music" from the throat of "an African singer." Moreover, to whom would Phillis, as "an African singer," relate? Most contemporary Blacks, including those very few who could read and write, were struggling for raw survival and had little time for literature not designed to ameliorate their conditions. Several Blacks (who may have been acquaintances of Phillis) retained lifelong fluency in their original African dialect. But, so far as whites were concerned, such a skill was useful only in helping to expedite early Black colonizing plans. The colonial press, however, might have indulged a short-lived exotic interest in the "songs" of Phillis as "an African singer." As for various modern belligerent Blacks who dismiss Phillis summarily, they are seemingly reacting to only a slight and traditionally under-representative portion of her work.

The foregoing comments do not mean to suggest that exhaustive research and textual analysis will one day reveal Phillis Wheatley to have been a cleverly disguised, badly misunderstood, militantly assertive Black woman. At the same time, there are quite clearly recognizable reasons why she has provoked, among Blacks and whites, such a controversial reputation. These reasons, reducible to so much white racism and reactionary Black chauvinism, include: white racist Colonial practices of the Christian religion; a white racist Colonial press; and a debilitating lack of any national sense of a self-respecting Black community, with the concomitant lack of a Black press. Despite these very real obstacles, however, Phillis Wheatley did indeed manage, in various ways, to have much more Black consciousness, much more concern for her fellow Blacks, than many readers will admit. She shows this awareness, this concern, both in her poetry, which was designed, it must be remembered, for a public (i.e., white) consideration, and more readily in her letters, designed for private attention.

Much has been written on the tremendous impact of the Christian religion on the Colonial American period. In one denomination or another, this religion was the single most powerful authoritative agent of those times. Christianity was made to serve as the fundamental reference for metaphysical and secular meaning and purpose in the white man's aesthetic, philosophical, and psychological relationships, including, of course, the Black slave-white master social relationship. While they could not avoid observing daily white racist practice of this religion, several of Phillis' articulate Black contemporaries persisted in following the written, idealized form of the faith. Jupiter Hammon (1711-1805?), Long Island-born and reared servant, published nothing but what have been regarded as pious placations. Likely a self-styled lay minister caught up in the Methodist fervor and secular white demands of his day, Hammon often found himself defensive because of what were thought to be his conciliatory notions about Black freedom. After fleeing with his master's family from Long Island while it was besieged by the British, and settling in Hartford, Connecticut, he published a 24-page pamphlet entitled "A/Winter Piece/Being A/Serious Exhortation,/ with a call to the/UNCONVERTED/and a short/CONTEMPLATION/on the/DEATH OF JESUS CHRIST/," to which is appended "A Poem for Children with Thoughts of Death" (1782). In the essay, Hammon makes clear both his feelings about temporal freedom and his strong religious views:

> My Brethren, many of us are seeking a temporal freedom, and I wish you may obtain it; remember that all power in heaven and on earth belongs to God: if we are slaves, it is by the permission of God, if we are free it must be by the power of the most high God. (page 9)

My dear Brethren, as it hath been reported that I had petitioned to the court of Hartford against freedom, I now solemnly declare that I never had said nor done anything, neither directly nor indirectly, to promote or to prevent freedom; but my answer hath always been I am a stranger here and I do not care to be concerned or to meddle with public affairs, and by this declaration I hope my friends will be satisfied and all prejudice removed. (page 9)

Espousing a popular, ineffectual philosophy, Hammon was clearly imbued with the Calvinist notion of man's utter helplessness in the hands of God. Such passivity did not sit well with his Black fellows, some veterans of war for human freedom. And today he is more remembered for the sentiments of his poem, "An Evening Thought" (1760), which establishes him as the first published Negro poet in America. Hammon chose Phillis Wheatley's widely circulated story to verify what he regarded as one more of God's divinely secular revelations. Long and wearisome—obvious and unvarying in sentiment and metrics—the poem is entitled "An Address to Miss Phillis Wheatly [sic] Ethiopian Poetess, in Boston, who came from Africa at eight years of age, and soon became acquainted with the gospel of Jesus Christ." The first two stanzas are representative enough:

1

O, come, you pious youth! adore
The wisdom of thy God,
In bringing thee from distant shore,
To learn His holy word.

2

Thou mightest been left behind,
Amid a dark abode;
God's tender mercy still combined,
Thou hast the holy word.

In later stanzas, Hammon asserts, as did other 18th century religious Blacks, his praise of Christian America and his denunciation of "heathen" Africa:

11

Thou hast left the heathen shore;
  Through mercy of the Lord;
Among the heathen live no more;
  Come magnify thy God.

17

While thousands muse with earthly toys,
  And range about the street,
Dear Phillis, seek for heaven's joys,
  Where we do hope to meet.

Hammon like, as we shall see, Phillis Wheatley, was not necessarily condemning Black Africa, as many readers easily conclude, so much as he was condemning "heathen" Africa. Nor was he (or Phillis) necessarily praising white America, but he seems to be praising Christian America. Both Hammon and Phillis were primarily concerned with Christianity as a philosophical-religious way of existence, but they were at the same time much aware of the hypocrisy of whites who falsely professed this religion. Hammon was appreciative of Black desire for civil liberty, as is seen in his 1782 speech and in a later address, ("An Address to the Negroes of the State of New York," 1786, 1787, 1806), where he speaks with either brilliantly muted irony or incredible naivétè:

> . . . *Now I acknowledge that liberty is a great thing, and worth seeking* for, if we can get it honestly, and by our good conduct prevail on our masters to set us free. Though for my own part I do not wish to be free: *yet I should be glad, if others, especially the young negroes were to be free,* for many of us are grown up slaves, and have always had masters to take care of us, should hardly know how to take care of ourselves; and it may be more for our own comfort to remain as we are. *That liberty is a great thing we may know from our own feelings, and we may likewise judge so from the conduct of the white people, in the late war. How much money has been spent, and how many lives have been lost to defend their liberty. I must say that I have hoped that God would open their eyes, when they were so much engaged for liberty, to think of the state of the poor blacks, and to pity us.* (italics mine)

Down in Philadelphia, another Black religious figure, Cryus Bustill (1732-1806), was exhorting sentiments somewhat similar to Hammon's. In his "Addrass [sic] to the Blacks in Philadelfiea [sic] 9th month 18th 1787," Bustill supplies an autobiographical account and goes on to his main points: He was born and reared a slave until he was

> almost 37 years of age, when it Please him out of his Great Marcey [sic] and his Still abounding Goodness, Towards me, to Plock [pluck] me out of the hands of unseasonable men and that at a time when I little Exspected [sic] it, ...
> . . . if we will but depart from Evil, you being in bondage in Particular, I would that [ye] take heed that afend [i.e., offend] not with your tongue, be ye wiss [wise] as Sarpants [sic] and harmless as Doves, that he may take with you, when you are wrong'd. . . . I would my Bretherin [sic] that, ye be faithful to your masters, at all times and on all ocasions [sic], too, for this is Praiseworthy, be honest and true to their intrust. Sappose [sic] they Do not See it the Great Master will see it and give Credit for it too, and therefore I would that ye Doe their business [with] Chairfulness [sic]. . . . Remember, if the Son make you free, you Shall be free indeed. . . .[50]

Meanwhile, in Phillis' Boston, Prince Hall (1748-1807) was urging the same kind of apparent passivity and dependence upon Christian serendipity to a handful of fellow Blacks. Rehearsing the duties of his newly formed Black Masons in "A Charge Delivered to the Brethren of the African Lodge, on the Twenty-Fifth of June, 1792, in Charlestown, by the R[ight] W[orshipful] Prince Hall," he admonished:

> But, in the meantime, let us lay by our recreations, and all superfluities, so that we may have that to educate our rising generations which was spent in these follies. Make you this beginning, and who knows but *God may raise up some friend or body of friends, as he did in Philadelphia, to open a school for blacks here, as that friendly city had done there.*[51] (italics mine)

There were other 18th century Blacks who, in varying degrees of conviction and fervor, looked to the Christian

God as one source of comfort for Black people at the capricious mercy of a hostile white society. Almost all, including Phillis Wheatley, recognized the practicality of including the Christian religion in plans to alleviate the Black man's plight. And unlike white Christians, who seemed to be praying for personal absolution from original sin, Black Christians prayed for group succor. The point is made in the words of John Marrant (1755-1792), a zealous Black Christian missionary who preached a sermon before Prince Hall's Masonic African Lodge No. 459 (later No. 370):

> . . . then what can these God-provoking wretches think, who despise their fellow man, as tho' they were not of the same species with themselves and would if in their power deprive them of *the blessings and comforts of this life, which God in his bountiful goodness hath freely given to all his creatures to enjoy?* [52]

Marrant strongly implies a Black notion that living on earth is or can be very much worthwhile; whereas many white Christians argued that earth is meant to be a continuously challenging place where only those worthy of afterlife are winnowed out.

There were countless reasons, spiritual, social, psychological, cultural, why early Black Americans took to the Christian religion, but easily among the more fundamental reasons was the compelling need to find some cohering factor to galvanize the scattered handfuls of almost completely disjointed, dependent Negroes into some kind of viable, meaningful community. By 1790 (six years after Phillis had died) there were in Philadelphia "about 250 [Black] families . . . making nearly 1000 persons, of both sexes, almost 450 of whom are minors." In Boston then there were only 766 free Negroes. In Philadelphia, Boston and other growing colonial cities, these free Negroes were largely confined to menial labor as cooks, bootblacks, laundresses, waiters, sweeps and "servants." And even these low-level jobs were held at the whim of white employers, obliging Negroes to develop a stronger relationship between themselves and their employers than they developed among their own family members.

Long humiliated by being confined to Jim Crow pews and by prejudicial treatment in white Christian churches, inevitably Blacks began to form their own associations, especially after Absalom Jones and Richard Allen were forcibly ejected from praying even in segregated quarters of the white St. George's Church in Philadelphia in 1787. Characteristic of early Black uses of Christianity, in Philadelphia, Boston, Newport, Rhode Island, and elsewhere, the rise of the Black church was not simplistically an ideologically reactionary affair: almost all Black American churches began with the founding of Black self-help mutual organizations. Examples include the "Free African Society" of Philadelphia, "The Union Society of Africans in Newport" (Obour Tanner's home), and "The African Meeting House" of Boston. Inspired by religious ideals, but tempered by practical considerations, these mutually beneficial groups were meant to cope with a range of abuses, their services including the dignified legitimization of Black marriages, medical care, especially for the Black aged and infirm, and even burials (in Philadelphia and Boston, Blacks were often buried in local Potters' fields).

These examples of early Black uses of the Christian religion clarify the point: while white Americans interpreted and implemented Christianity for one selfish end, colonial Blacks, including Phillis Wheatley, were vigorously interpreting and, as subtly and effectively as they could, implementing Christianity for humane, Blacker ends.

All of this does not mean that, throughout the 18th century, no Blacks were more overtly, more dramatically protesting slavery and racial prejudice, including outright militancy. But, in the 18th century especially, Black protest ordinarily found no expression in the racist colonial newspapers, which were practically house organs for early American capitalists. During Phillis Wheatley's lifetime in Boston, New England seaports became the very hub of America's thriving slave trade. Although all of the New England states had eradicated slavery within their own boundaries during her Boston lifetime (Vermont, 1777; New Hampshire, 1780; Massachusetts, 1783; Connecticut, 1784; Rhode Island, 1784), the American slave traffic was firmly in the grasp of New Englanders from 1638, when at Marblehead, Massachusetts, was built the *Desire*, the first American-built ship specifically designed for the African slave trade, to February 21, 1862, when Captain Nathaniel Gordon, of Portland, Maine, was convicted and hanged in New York as a pirate dealing in the then illegal traffic. By 1770, for instance, Rhode Island alone had one hundred and fifty vessels in the African slave trade. "This trade," wrote Samuel Hopkins, "has been the first wheel of commerce in Newport, on which every other movement in business depended. That town has built up, and flourished in the past on slave trade," and by it the inhabitants "have gotten most of their wealth and riches."[53] Small fortunes for average businessmen could be made by funding a single successful slave voyage or two.

It is little wonder that these businessmen, these potential newspaper readers and advertisers, would discourage the colonial press from printing stinging indictments of their way of life. Difficult as it might have been for a Black protester to publish his feelings in that press, even white men of prominence were denied access if their views were regarded as outrageous. The eminent but outspoken anti-slavery advocate, Reverend Samuel Hopkins of Newport, found strong resistance and failed to have his "Dialogue Concerning the Slavery of the Africans, together with his address to Slaveholders" (1776) appear in the Newport press, because that press "would not safely engage in so offensive an enterprise."[54] It finally appeared in a more congenial Norwich, Connecticut publication. Anti-slavery protests were printed, to be sure, but they were mostly condemnations of the obviously brutal aspects of the system, and they were usually written by white persons. The very few pieces of protest that were written by Blacks and published in colonial times were done with a full knowledge that "as free speech was not then exactly established as the right of all men, these men had to write under assumed names."[55] A certain "Othello" published an essay, "Negro Slavery," in 1788, and "A Free Negro" published "Slavery" the next year. Although "Othello" is said to have been a Negro, this identification may be questioned when he affects such sentiment as

> Yet when *we* take *them* from Africa, *we* deprive *them* of a country which God hath Given *them* for *their* own, as free as *we* are, and as capable of enjoying that blessing. Like pirates *we* go to commit devastation on the coast of an innocent country, and among a people who never did *us* wrong.[56] (italics mine)

It was not until the 19th century, with the founding of the Negro press in John Russwurm's *Freedom's Journal* (1827), that Blacks found publishing outlets for their more freely acknowledged protests. During Phillis' time, there were, of course, some few written Black protests. Aptheker documents several 18th century statements of varying vehemence, but, as can be gathered from their titles—*To his Excellency Thomas Gage, Esq. Captain General and Governor Chief over this Province; To the Honorable Counsel & House of Representatives for the State of Massachusetts Bay in General Court Assembled, January 13, 1777;* etc.—they were not designed for publication in the colonial press. They were, rather, petitions to various legislatures; and as such they became state papers, and would likely have remained in obscure state archives or college libraries if Aptheker had not published them as late as 1951. On a very few occasions the colonial press did publish Negro-written material of "an approved and acceptable" nature, something, for instance, like the ostensibly Negro-written piece of exotica advertised in the Newport (R.I.) *Mercury* on August 22, 1774: *A/Narrative/of the /Most Remarkable Particulars/in the/Life/of James Albert Ukasaw Gronniosaw,/An African Prince/Written by Himself*. The book in fact, as the 1770 edition states, "was *related* by himself." The narrative recounts the remarkable life of an enslaved scion of a royal African family who must watch his English wife and their three children sharing a single carrot a day for several days; it does not so much protest slavery as it emphasizes the happy intervention in his life of Christian compassion.

If Phillis Wheatley had been of a fiery, militant persuasion, the colonial press would not have welcomed her written charges. Whether Phillis published her work in single broadsides, in newspapers and magazines, or as a collected volume, it went through important editorial changes. Different versions of the same poem are, of course, the result of her own revisions. Mason finds that "for seven of her poems we have revised versions which show that she could improve . . ."; but he also feels that "she probably did not revise all of her poems, certainly did not revise most of them much, and obviously should have revised more."[57] What Mason says has its truth, and yet a consideration of some of the revisions strongly indicates that Phillis, to an unrealized extent, knew that she was Black in a white-styled world, despite the relative liberalism of Abolitionist-minded England.

For example, her widely celebrated poem "On The Death of the Rev. Mr. George Whitefield" was reprinted in Boston, Newport, Philadelphia, New York and London at least ten times, but there are more than syntactical, grammatical and metrical revisions found in the 1771 London edition. Dedicated to the eccentric, reformist Countess of Huntingdon, the London version contains a reference not found in a single one of the many American versions: the word "free" (line 44) in the plain and obvious sense of the word. In the 1770 American broadside version, there are 62 lines, lines 35-44 of which paraphrase the late evangelist's urging to assemblies:

> Take HIM ye wretched for your only good;
> Take HIM ye starving souls to be your food,
> Ye thirsty, come to his life giving stream:
> Ye Preachers, take him for your joyful theme:
> Take HIM, "my dear AMERICANS," he said,
> Be your complaints in his kind bosom laid:

Take HIM ye AFRICANS, he longs for you;
Impartial SAVIOUR, is his title due;
If you will chuse to walk in grace's road,
You shall be sons, and kings, and priests to God

In the 1773 American version, reduced to 47 lines, the same paraphrasing (lines 28-37) reads:

"Take him, ye wretched, for your only good,
"Take him ye starving sinners, for your food;
"Ye thirsty, come to this life-giving stream,
"Take him my dear *Americans,*" he said,
"Be your complaints on his kind bosom laid:
"Take him, ye *Africans,* he longs for you,
"*Impartial Saviour* is his title due:
"Wash'd in the fountain of redeeming blood,
"You shall be sons, and kings, and priests to God."

However, only the paraphrasing, beginning at line 35 in the 64-line English version of the poem, contains the most important of all the changes she made to the piece:

Take him, ye Wretched, for your only Good:
Take him, ye hungry Souls, to be your Food;
Take him, ye Thirsty, for your cooling Stream;
Ye Preachers, take him for your joyful Theme;
Take him, my dear *Americans,* he said
Be your complaints in his kind Bosom laid;
Take him, ye Africans, he longs for you
Impartial Saviour is his Title due.
If you will walk in Grace's heavenly Road,
He'll make you *free,* and Kings, and Priests to God. (italics in last line mine)

In this London version, Phillis exhibits her own way of soliciting the powerful and the friendly to demonstrate compassion for her less fortunate fellow Blacks. The deliberate use of the word "free' also is one more instance of the communal uses to which early Black typically subjected Christianity.

Phillis evidently felt that she could be more self-assertive in her London poems, for she sent, with a covering letter to the Earl of Dartmouth, a poem that has since been recognized as her most outspoken piece of Black protest: "To The Right Honourable William, Earl of Dartmouth, His Majesty's Principal Secretary of State of North America, &." The manuscript of the poem has not yet turned up, but there is strong likelihood that it differed from the version published in her 1773 collection. Even there, the poem is forthright in establishing Phillis' particular right to versify proclamations concerning human freedom, as can be seen from an excerpt:

> Should you, my lord, while you peruse my song,
> Wonder from whence my love of Freedom sprung,
> Whence flow these wishes for the common good,
> By feeling hearts alone best understood,
> I, young in life, by seeming cruel fate
> Was snatch'd from Africa's fancy'd happy seat:
> What pangs excrutiating must molest,
> What sorrows labour in my parent's breast?
> Steel'd was that soul and by no misery mov'd
> That from a father seiz'd his babe belov'd:
> Such, such my case. And can I then but pray
> Others may never feel tyrannic sway?

While preparing an exhibition of Negro History at the Library Company of Philadelphia, librarian Robert Kuncio discovered, in the collection of the Library Company and in the collection of the Historical Society of Pennsylvania, five manuscript poems by the talented Boston Black poet. One had been printed in the 1773 volume, but "to my knowledge," wrote Kuncio in 1970, "the four remaining verses, and a contemporary copy of one of them, had not been published."[57] Published and annotated by Kuncio, these poems are "To the King's Most excellent Majesty on his repealing the american [sic] Stamp Act" (in revised form in the 1773 volume); "On the death of Mr. Snider Murder'd by Richardson"; "America"; "Atheism"; and "To the honble. Commodore Hood on his pardoning a deserter"; and "on Atheism," a contemporary copy of "Atheism." Largely from internal references, Kuncio reckons that all of these undated poems "were composed between 1768 and 1770."[58] Since these patriotic poems were likely composed early in her career, a question arises as to why she did not choose any more than one of them to be included in her 1773 volume. Kuncio points to one obvious answer.

"In the Stamp Act poem, the changes in the printed copy bear out the position that Phillis Wheatley's 'patriotic' poems may have been withheld or altered for matters politics."[59] Kuncio is even nearer the truth when he states: "It is this interest in liberty that may have made it politic to exclude two of the . . . poems from the volume published in London, and that may have made an unknown editor or Miss Wheatley herself alter a third when it was later printed. . . ."[60]

There were indeed "censors" to much, if not all, of Phillis' poetry. Miss Wheatley wrote most of her eulogistic and patriotic and even occasional poems for specific persons, often at their prompting or solicitation, and these persons saw to it that her work was or was not published, depending on the personal or political wisdom in so doing. For instance, her patriotic poem, "On The Capture of General Lee," dated in its manuscript "Boston, Dec. 30, 1776," remained in manuscript for almost ninety years before being first printed by the Massachusetts Historical Society in 1863-64. A prefatory note explains:

> The President of the Massachusetts Historical Society said that he had found among the Bowdoin Papers the original manuscript of a poem by the celebrated negro [sic] slave, Phillis Wheatley, on the capture of General Charles Lee by the British. It has never been printed, so far as he could ascertain. It was certainly not in either of the editions of the printed volumes of her poems. He then read it as follows.[61]

The 70-line paean praises General Green as a dedicated American Revolutionary hero, lured into capture by deceptively gracious British Officers. Invited to be a guest in the British camp, Lee is made to utter poetic heroics:

> Thus spoke the foe; and warlike Lee reply'd,
> "Ill fits it me, who such an army guide,
> To whom his conduct each brave solider owes,
> To waste an hour in banquet or repose:

This day important, with loud voice demands
Our wisest Counsels, and our bravest hands."

Once in the British camp, Lee is told that he is a prisoner, but he persists in his versified gallantries, which include elaborate praise of General Washington, praise not elsewhere documented:

While thus he spoke the hero of renown
Survey'd the boaster with a gloomy frown,
And stern reply'd: "Oh arrogance of tongue!
And wild ambition, ever prone to wrong!
Believ'st thou chief, that armies such as thine
Can stretch in dust that heaven-defended line?
In vain allies may swarm from distant lands,
And demons aid in formidable bands. . . .
What various causes to the field invite!
For plunder *you,* and we for freedom fight. . . .
Already, thousands of your troops are fled
To the drear mansions of the silent dead:
Columbia too, beholds with streaming eyes
Her heroes fall—'tis freedom's sacrifice! . . .
Yet those brave troops innum'rous as the sands
One soul inspires, one General Chief commands.
Find in your train of boasted heroes, one
To match the praise of Godlike Washington.
Thrice happy Chief! in whom the virtues join,
And heaven-taught prudence speaks the man divine!"

Phillis has been chastised for writing this poem "hardly in keeping with the facts."[62] The facts include the known hostility which General Charles Lee (1731-1782) harbored for General Washington, whom he joined as the appointed second ranking major general late in 1776. Constantly insulting Washington and even dangerously jeopardizing the outcome of the war, Lee was captured near Monmouth, New Jersey, and remained captive until 1778, during which time he planned strategy for the British to capture Washington's forces. When he was exchanged in 1778, he continued in command—his traitorous plans not being discovered until 1858—and continued insulting Washington, until finally he was court-martialed and discharged from the service. While it is true that Phillis would not have access to such high-level goings-on, it must be remembered also that Lee was captured on December 13, 1776, and Phillis' tributary poems to him was dated December 30, 1776. That Phillis did not know of these Lee-Washington confrontations may well have been "why Bowdoin never let the poem be published,"[63] but that she was that much at odds with the facts is something else again.

Another instance of Phillis' work being subjected to "beneficent intermediaries" (or censors) can be found in a note written by someone identified only as "L" and in a second note written by Phillis, both of which preface her poem "Recollection,/To Miss A—M—, humbly inscribed by the Authoress." The note read:

> To the Author of the London Magazine./Boston, in New-England, Jan 1, 1772./SIR,/As your Magazine is a proper repository for anything valuable or curious, I hope you will excuse the communicating the following by one of your subscribers./L./There is in this town a young *Negro woman,* who left *her* country at ten years of age, and has been in *this* eight years. She is a compleat sempstress, an accomplished mistress of her pen, and discovers a most surprising genius. Some of her productions have seen the light, among which is a poem on the death of the Rev. Mr. George Whitefield.— The following was occasioned by her being in company with some young ladies of family, when one of them said she did not remember, among all the poetical pieces she had seen, ever to have met with a poem upon RECOLLECTION. The *African* (so let me call her, for so in fact she is) took the hint, went home to her master's, and soon sent what follows.
>
> "MADAM,
>
> Agreeable to your proposing *Recollection as a subject proper for me to write upon,* I enclose these few thoughts upon it; and, as you was the first person who mentioned it; I thought none more proper to dedicate it to; and, *if it meets with your approbation,* the poem is honoured, and the authoress satisfied. I am, Madam,
>
> Your very humble servant
> PHILLIS."
>
> (except for the word *Recollection,* italics in Phillis' letters are mine)[64]

Thus it can be seen that, in addition to contending with a hostile white colonial press, Phillis had to please the various persons for whom she composed her pieces. But these were not all of Phillis' problems: she also had to contend with indifferent editors, and especially uninformed anthologizers of her work. Her editors claim to reprint "the original edition" of her 1773 volume, but there are decided differences not only between later editions and the 1773 volume, but among later editions themselves. Some differences appear slight and may be attributable to printers' carelessness, although omissions of whole lines from various poems may have been deliberate. Brawley, for instance, noted that several early editors "unfortunately omit line 17 of the poem 'To the University of Cambridge, in New England.'" To mention only a few other such variances, in the 1802 (Walpole, New Hampshire) edition, line 15 of "To the University of Cambridge, in New England," and line 64 of "Thoughts on the Works of Providence" are missing; in the 1834 (George W. Light, Boston) edition, line 17 of "To the University of Cambridge, in New England" is missing. In the 1838 (Isaac Knapp, Boston) edition, there is a facsimile of Phillis' engraved likeness, but the facsimile has endowed Phillis with deeply wavy hair. Along with inevitable printers' "corrections" and "modernizations" of the original spelling and punctuation, other discrepancies and omissions in other editions can be found.

By now one may have grown accustomed to various white editors' and anthologizers' indifferent attention to Black literature, but it is surprising to note the cavalier treatment given to Phillis' work by ranking Black authors. In 1927, Countee Cullen published *Caroling Dusk: An Anthology of Verse by Negro Poets,* in which Phillis Wheatley is not represented at all. Says Cullen:

> The student of verse by American Negro poets will find *in these three anthologies* comprehensive treatment of the works of Negro poets from Phyllis [sic] Wheatley, the first American Negro known to have composed verses, to writers of the present day. (italics mine)[65]

"These three anthologies" are James Weldon Johnson's *The Book of American Negro Poetry* (1922); Robert T. Kerlin's *Negro Poets and Their Poems* (1923); and *An Anthology of Verse by American Negroes,* edited by Newman I. White and Walter C. Jackson in 1924. The comprehensiveness of the treatment of Phillis in these anthologies, singly or collectively, is questionable. Johnson's pioneering anthology in its original (1922) and revised and expanded (1931) edition has demonstrated its literary value, and is especially brilliant in its lengthy critical introduction. Nevertheless, Johnson's treatment of Phillis consists of a lively enough *discussion* of her poetic merits, but he presents only a 10-line example of her actual work, 10 lines from the 53-line "On Imagination." Kerlin's book includes not a single illustrative line by Phillis, while White and Jackson include only three poems (one being the entire "On Imagination) and 2 lines from a fourth poem. The total number of Phillis' poems represented by all three books together is 3, so it is difficult to grasp what Cullen meant by "comprehensive treatment" of Phillis' works.

Both Cullen and Johnson had, somehow, overlooked the critically important *The Negro in Literature and Art in the United States* (1918), by Benjamin Brawley. Brawley, the first major Black critic to give appropriate attention to Phillis, here devotes to her twenty-three pages of reasoned commentary, including generous excerpts from her letters, then little known, plus a four-page bibliographical essay. Yet, her only poetry in this helpful volume is the 8-line "On Being Brought From Africa to America," the first 10 lines of "On Imagination" and 4 lines from "On Virtue." A white anthologizer, Vernon Loggins, in his thorough-going *The Negro Author, His Development in America to 1900* (1931, 1959, 1964), also uses more discussion than poetic excerpts. He includes 8 and 12 lines from her poems, their virtue being that they had not been widely anthologized before. Not until 1935 was Phillis Wheatley represented in a generous and illustrative manner, in Benjamin Brawley's *Early Negro American Writers,* which offers 10 complete poems.

The point, in referring to these earlier anthologies, is to note that until 1935 perhaps no more than 12 or 14 of Phillis' poems had been anthologized in excerpted and complete versions. Many samplings were repeatedly anthologized later. However, it is known that, to date, there are almost 60 published poems by this woman in her own lifetime, and there are extant 18 letters. 22 letters, really, with the recent publication of Kenneth Silverman, "Four New Letters by Phillis Wheatley," Early American Literature, VIII, No. 3 (Winter, 1974) 257-271, which article was brought to my attention only after the present work was completed. It must also be remembered that by 1779, Phillis had written even more poems and letters, enough to war-
by subscribing in advance, would underwrite printing ex-
rant her collecting them and advertising for persons who,
penses for a second volume of poems and letters. The chaos provoked by the war and its unsettling aftermath obliged persons, even persons of some means, to consider survival more than the encouragement, and thus the projected vol-
has been noted, was returned to her husband upon his de-
ume was never published. The manuscript of this volume, as
mand, and he "some years after . . . went to the South. . . ." What became of the manuscript is still unknown, although one recent source says: "The MSS., however, are still in existence; they are owned by an accomplished citizen of Philadelphia, whose Mother was one of the patrons of the author."[66] A speculation follows: "The accomplished citizen was probably James Rush."[67]

Phillis' proposals for a second volume listed 33 titles of poems and 13 titles of letters. It is known that 2 and likely 4 of the 33 poems have been published, and it is also clear that at least 4 of the 13 letters have been published. Mason publishes 16 "new" pieces (including 7 early versions of poems later revised and published); Robert C. Kuncio has unearthed 6 hitherto unpublished verses (including an early version of a poem later revised and published, and including 2 versions of another poem on "Atheism"); Carl Bridenbaugh has printed what is likely Phillis' first published poem; Lorenzo Greene presents one of several versions of "Atheism"; I have published 8 other poems (including, herewith, 2 more manuscript versions of "On Atheism," making a total of 5 different versions of a single poem; see Appendix). With either 31 or 29 poems still in manuscript, there is a grand total of over 100 poems known to have been written by Phillis. Even considering that several of the published poems are earlier versions of poems later revised; and that likely 4 of her advertised poems have been published along with some 22 letters and notes, this is still a remarkable achievement for Phillis Wheatley. Moreover, others of her poems and letters occasionally turn up. Clearly, then, it is gross unfairness to reach definite conclusions about such a precocious young Black colonial woman without some consideration of the entire bulk she produced in some 17-odd years of writing.

Because she has not been fully represented in anthologies, the poet's reputation has suffered, and her true posture has not been entirely explained. It has been charged, for instance, that Phillis

> wrote too rarely about herself. Her intimate personal interests were ignored. She composed verses on the deaths of those who meant little to her. . . ."[68]

These remarks reveal scant consideration of the racist realities of Phillis' times. We have already seen the reason Phillis did not poeticize her feelings about Mrs. Wheatley's death. Specifically,

> It appears, also, that on her deathbed she requested that nothing might be written upon her decease. Indeed, Phillis was forbidden this indulgence of her grief, and it was shortly after her mournful duty to close the eyes of her indulgent mistress and unwearied friend.[69]

We have also seen that Phillis, while obliging her mistress, did not write any poems about that matter, but did record her grief in the confidence of a letter to her friend in Newport, fellow Black domestic Obour Tanner. We have seen that the Colonial press was not amenable to publication of forceful anti-slavery protests, especially those written by Black persons, and that there was not a viable Black community to support or buy any privately printed protest broadsides that Phillis or any other 18th century Black might have composed. The notion that "she composed verses on the deaths of those who meant little to her" might also be examined.

Phillis, as an occasional poet, often commemorated the death of a relative of a friend or of some ranking personality. There are almost two dozen such eulogistic pieces among Phillis' works, with such titles as "On the Death of a Young Lady of Five Years of Age"; "On the Death of a Young Gentleman"; "To A Lady on the Death of Three Relations"; "To A Lady and Her Children, on the Death of Her Son and Their Brother." The poems, in keeping with the generality of Neo-Classical poetics give little biographical information about the "ladies." But titles of several of these poems in her 1773 volume are revisions of earlier, relatively more detailed titles: e.g., "To A Lady on the Death of Her Husband" (1773) is a revision of the earlier "To Mrs. Leonard on the Death of Her Husband" (1771); "To A Clergyman on the Death of his Lady" (1773) first appeared as "To the Rev. Mr. Pitkin, on the Death of His Lady" (1772); and "A Funeral Poem on the Death of C.E. an Infant of Twelve Months (1773) is a revised version of "A Poem on the Death of Charles Eliot aged 12 Months" (1772); "To the Honourable T. H. Esq: On the Death of his Daughter" (1773) was originally entitled "To the Hon'ble Thomas Hubbard, Esq.: On the Death of Mrs. Thankfull Leonard" (1773, January 2). Phillis Wheatley then revised generally toward a definite end: conformity with Neo-Classical poetic demands. She knew very well that most Americans, unfamiliar and perhaps even unconcerned with Neo-Classical aesthetics, wanted their poetry to be more specific and concrete, at least to include their own names in the titles. She knew too that in England, where her volume would likely be more critically scrutinized, readers would expect more emphasis on the typical, the general, the "universal." In her poetry not in the 1773 volume, which is to say in her poetry published about and for American readers, she *is* relatively detailed, specific. Consider the following titles of poems not in her 1773 collection: "AN ELEGY,/To Miss Mary Moorhead, on the DEATH/of her Father, The REV. Mr./JOHN MOORHEAD"; "AN ELEGY,/ SACRED TO THE MEMORY OF THAT/GREAT DIVINE,/THE REVEREND AND LEARNED/DR. SAMUEL COOPER,/"; "On Messrs. HUSSEY and COFFIN (1767)"; "On the Death of Mr. Snider Murder'd by Richardson." Any examination of the charge that Phillis did "compose verses on the deaths of those who meant little to her" must try to determine just who these subjects were, and how they related to Phillis personally and/or to the colonial Black condition generally.

It ought to be understood that, while many Blacks were unhappy with their status but powerless to overthrow it, slavery was generally accepted during most of Phillis' Boston lifetime. There were Indian and white men and women held in legal servitude as indentured servants and as slaves. Phillis has been called obsequious and fawningly ingratiating because she wrote poems for several eminent personalities who were slave-traders and slaveholders. But consideration of the facts of her time—the settled idea of universal inferiority for the Black man and woman; the lack of a Black community strong enough to challenge and destroy such notions; only a vaguely stirring handful of white sympathizers—will show that Phillis was much aware of her colonial realities and was appealing to the daily touted ostensible Christian morality of various personalities, several of whom were, in practical fact, helpful to indigent Blacks even while firmly believing in racial superiority. The hypocritical ambiguities and existential dilemma of being Black in a white world, still known today, were even more severe in Phillis' times.

Supplying biographical data for persons identifiable in Phillis' poems is tangential to the purposes at hand, but a glance at a selection of these persons will show that the poet, fully aware of racial hypocrisy, might well have been appealing to the broadcast Christian compassion of whites, on behalf of Blacks in and out of slavery. For instance, Phillis has been chastised for poetically eulogizing George Whitefield (1714-1770), who, for all of his overwhelmingly popular evangelizing, nevertheless did use, and speciously rationalize the use of, slave labor for the erection of his orphanage in Bethesda, Georgia. But it should be more widely known that he "took up 5000 Acres of land on the forks of Delaware, in the Province of Pennsylvania, in order to erect a Negro school there. . . ."[70] Phillis' eulogy might easily have reflected her knowledge of Whitefield's planned school. Her poem "On Messrs. HUSSEY and COFFIN" (1767) concerns old Nantucket merchant Quaker families, who, like most New England Quakers, boasted of their fair dealings with Indians and Blacks. It is known that her "To a Gentleman on His Voyage to Great-Britain For the Recovery of His Health" is really "addressed to Joseph Rotch, a brother of William Rotch, Sr., both members of the prominent merchant family of the same name of New Bedford and Nantucket,"[71] but it has not been noted that Joseph and William Rotch's sister, Elizabeth Rotch Rodman, "was a friend of the slave, and interested in every cause of humanity."[72] Her poem "To the Hon'ble Thomas Hubbard, Esq.: On the Death of Mrs. Thankfull Leonard" (1771) involved the Thomas Hubbard who was "a member of the Old South Church for forty-three years. . . . He left 200 pounds to the poor of Boston, and 50 pounds to the Charitable and Pious fund of the Old South."[73] Phillis was a member of the Old South church after 1771, and it does not strain credulity to deduce that she was poetically thanking a man who considered the Boston poor, and it is a safe presumption that many Blacks were among this number.

It is perfectly true that most of the eighteen "most respectable characters in Boston" whose names preface Phillis' 1773 volume dealt in some way with the slave trade, or even owned slaves. But it is also true that "slavery" in the New England of Phillis' time was not to be compared to slavery in the South:

> New England slave trade was small and was marked neither by the drama nor the cruelty associated with the latter. . . . Legally, the New England slave had a position somewhere between that of a plantation slave and an indentured servant. This was due to the influence of Jewish slavery after which the Puritans patterned their system of involuntary servitude. The New England slave was in a measure a member of his master's family and, following the Hebraic tradition, was usually referred to as "servant," rarely as slave. Holding this intermediate status, Negroes were considered as both property and as persons before the law; hence their legal status was never rigidly fixed. As property, Negroes were bought, sold, transferred, included in wills, inventories and deeds, and other personal estate. They were escheated to the town if the master died intestate and without heirs. Slaves might also be seized or sold to satisfy legal claims brought against themselves or their masters. Slaves were at the same time considered to be persons and as such could acquire, receive, hold, administer and transfer property. They could also sue and be sued and they had the right of appeal to the highest colonial courts. As persons, moreover, they enjoyed virtually the same rights before the courts as did free white persons. They possessed the right of trial both by the grand and petit juries; they could pass upon their trial jurors, and could offer testimony against white persons in the courts in cases not involving Negroes. . . .[74]

Too vastly complex for thorough explication in these few pages, colonial New England slavery seems, simplistically put, to have engendered a relationship in which the "unfortunate weak" (some few whites but mostly Blacks) were thrown into dependency upon the "fortunate strong" (some few Blacks, but mostly whites). There were free Blacks, of course, some of them even owning slaves themselves, but they were not automatically among the "fortunate strong." On the contrary, being Black and free often enforced wretched lifestyles. As one scholar has noted, "Economically, the status of the free Negro was inferior to that of the slaves. Whereas in slavery every type of employment was open to them, in freedom, faced with the combined competition of slaves, indentured servants and free white workmen, the freedmen were confined by circumstances largely to domestic service."[75] Thus, ironical as it must seem to modern sensibility, some colonial Blacks regarded themselves as indeed fortunate if they could secure a remunerative position with the likes of those people whose names preface Phillis' 1773 volume. Such a relationship meant to the desperate Black—whatever his status might be called, servant or slave—the assurance of room and board and protection and even incidental enjoyment of whatever prestige a powerful master might command.

Phillis took recourse to such prestige when she found great difficulty having her volume published in this country. There being too many whites who could not believe that a Black person could produce such work and on such a scale, Phillis remanded her poems from the American printers and drew upon the reputation she enjoyed among the prominent citizens of Boston who signed the note of attestation she had drawn up. She could then assure the volume's publication, and in London, where it would stimulate more prestige and sales than would an American edition. The situation is referred to in a contemporary letter dated "Boston, 24, Feb'y, 1773," written by a John Andrews to a William Barrell in Philadelphia. Andrews points out, in part:

> In regard to Phillis' poems they will/originate from a London press, as she was [blam'd] by her friends for printing them here & made to expect a large emolument if she sent the copy home [i.e., to England], which induc'd her to remand it of the printers & also [?]/of Cap't. Calef, who [could] not sell it by reason of their/not crediting the performance to be a Negro, since/which she has [illegible] papers drawn up & sign'd by/the Gov. Council, Ministers of most of the people of/note in this place, certifying the authenticity of it;/which paper Cap't. Calef carried last fall, therefore/we/may expect it in print by the Spring ships, it is/supposed the copy will sell for 100 pound Sterling. . . .[76]

It is this same Andrews who, in another letter to Barrell, dated "Boston, Jan., 28, 1774," made clear that Phillis might have been planning a second volume as early as 1774:

> . . . After so long a time have at last got Phillis' poems in

print, which will be [illegible] you by Cap't. Dunn, in a Brig Ben has the care of, these don't seem to be near all her productions, She's an [artful?] jade, I believe, & intends to have the benefit of another volume. . . .[77]

In this volume, it has been suggested, Phillis was not as personal or specific or detailed as some critics would prefer. But her obvious emulation of the Neo-Classical literary school—that 18th century English revival of what was believed to have been the ancient Greek philosophical mode of reasoned, moderated expression—required that she reflect a settled world of generalized, not particularized, humanity. There had to be restraint, decorum, balance and, above all, no exhibition of the poet's personal feelings, especially feelings about one particular subject or person. Dr. Samuel Johnson, a practitioner of Neo-Classicism, put it best when he said, "The business of a poet . . . is to examine, not the individual, but the species; to remark general properties and large appearances; he does not number the streaks of the tulip, or describe the different shades of the verdure of the forest. . . ."
Neo-Classical conventions of regularized generality were ultimately applied to the poetic line (iambic pentameter), to couplets, and to metaphors, similes, epithets, and references to classical gods and legends. Repeatedly, Phillis shows clearly her aspirations to write after the Neo-Classical manner, as in her undeveloped, unelaborated invocations to the ancient muses:

While an intrinsic ardor prompts to write,
The muses promise to assist my pen;
("To the University of Cambridge, in New England")
YE martial power's and all ye tuneful nine,
Inspire my song, and aid my high design.
The dreadful scenes and toils of war I write,
The ardent warriors, and the fields of fight:
You best remember, and you best can sing
The acts of heroes to the vocal string:
Resume the lays with which your sacred lyre,
Did then the poet and the sage inspire.
("Goliath of Gath")

MNEME begin. Inspire, ye sacred nine,
Your vent'rous *Afric* in her great design.
Mneme, immortal pow'r. I trace thy spring:
Assist my strains, while I thy glories sing.
("On Recollection")

Celestial muse! for sweetness fam'd inspire
My wondrous theme with true poetic fire,
("To a Gentleman of the Navy")

Again, in accordance with the Neo-Classical insistence on generality, she avoids describing the specific and instead presents the generic, so that "birds" becomes "the feather'd race" and "plants" becomes "sons of vegetation" which "spread their leafy banners to the skies." Phillis also favors her Neo-Classical masters' use of personification:

Among the mental pow'rs a question rose,
"What most the image of th' Eternal shows?"
When thus to *Reason* (so let *Fancy* rove)
Her great companion spoke, immortal *Love.*
("Thoughts on the Works of Providence")

Despite the fact that Phillis wrote within the confines of the Neo-Classical tradition, she was occasionally able to convey her very own enthusiasm, and she certainly engendered several lines of verse which are still memorable for their power and originality of expression:

As reason's pow'rs by day our God disclose,
So may we trace him in the night's repose:
Say what is sleep? and dreams how passing strange!
When action ceases, and ideas range
Licentious and unbounded o'er the plains.
Where's *Fancy's* queen in giddy triumph reigns,
Hear in soft strains the dreaming lover sigh
To a kind fair, or rave in jealousy;
On pleasure now, and now on vengeance bent,
The lab'ring passions struggle for a vent.
What pow'r, O man! thy reason then restores,
So long suspended in nocturnal hours?
What secret hand returns the mental train,
And gives improv'd thine active pow'rs again?
From thee, O man, what gratitude should rise!

And, when from balmy sleep thou op'st thine eyes,
Let thy first thoughts be praises to the skies.
How merciful our God who thus imparts
O'erflowing tides of joy to human hearts,
When wants and woes might be our righteous lot,
Our God forgetting, by our God forgot!
("Thoughts on the Works of Providence")

Also, she can be especially effective in her verses about death, a theme which, as popular eulogizer, she often treated:

On *Death's* domain intent I fix my eyes,
Where human nature in vast ruin lies:
With pensive mind I search the dreary abode,
Where the great conqu'rer has his spoils, bestow'd:
There, there the offspring of six thousand years
In endless numbers to my view appears:
Whole kingdoms in his gloomy den are thrust,
And nations mix with their primeval dust:
Insatiate still he gluts the ample tomb;
His is the present, his the age to come.
See here a brother, here a sister spread,
And a sweet daughter mingled with the dead. . . .
("To a Gentleman and Lady on the Death of the Lady's Brother and Sister, and a Child of the Name Avis, Aged One Year")

We trace the pow'r of Death from tomb to tomb,
And his are all the ages yet to come.
'Tis his to call the planets from on high,
To blacken *Phoebus,* and dissolve the sky;
His too, when all in his dark realms are hurl'd,
From its firm base to shake the solid world;
His fatal sceptre rules the spacious whole,
And trembling nature rocks from pole to pole.
Awful he moves, and wide his wings are spread:
("To a Lady on the Death of Three Relations")

Phillis used several memorable metaphors. One that has retained its power over the years can be found in the bravado uttered by the Biblical David as he confronts Goliath:

David undaunted thus, "Thy spear and shield
"Shall no protection to thy body yield:

"*Jehovah's* name — no other arms I bear,
I ask no other in this glorious war.
"Today the Lord of Hosts to me will give
"Vict'ry, to-day thy doom thou shalt receive:
"*And beasts shall be your animated tomb.* . . .
("Goliath of Gath./I Sam. Chap. XVII";
italics in last line mine)

By the play of synecdoche (the use of the whole of something for the part, or, more usually, the use of a significant part of something for the whole), she poeticizes how quickly the forests of Albion (i.e., England) are converted into sailing ships for the Royal Navy:

Far in the space where ancient Albion keeps
Amidst the roarings of the sacred deeps,
Where willing forests leave their native plain,
Descend, and instant, plough the wat'ry main.
Strange to relate! with canvas wings they speed
To distant worlds; of distant worlds the dread.
("To a Gentleman of the Navy"; italics mine)

There are other equally impressive passages. Indeed, on occasions, few enough to be sure, Phillis wrote poems that were completely successful, for instance, the widely anthologized "On Imagination," about which Brawley has said, it "is not only the best in this pseudo-neo-classical vein but probably from any standpoint the strongest poem in the book."[78]

But she could express her personal feelings, her racial self-consciousness, in other ways. Arthur Davis has already documented many of her personal and Black references throughout her work,[79] yet there are more. In varying degrees and ways, Phillis was indeed personal and persistently racially aware. The major themes of her poems concern patriotism and piety, sometimes conveyed through Biblical paraphrase; there were also some set pieces ("An Hymn to the Morning," "An Hymn to the Evening," etc.), all of her work stemming from an orthodox morality. Withal she let it be known that she was Black.

Often she would assume the conventionally deferential poetic posture of being in need of inspiration from the muses, but she often included, in this pose, tags of her racial identity. Thus she writes in a vainly pious exhortation to unruly Harvard University students of 1767:

Improve your privileges while they stay,
Ye pupils, and each hour redeem, that bears
Or good or bad report of you to heav'n.
Let sin, that baneful evil to the soul,
By you be shunn'd, nor once remit your guard;
. . . Ye blooming planets of human race devine, [sic]
An *Ethiop* tells you 'tis your greatest foe;
("To the University of Cambridge, in New England")

And in early religious joust with non-believers of her day:

Must Ethiopians be employ'd for you?
Much I rejoice if any good I do.
I ask O unbeliever, Satan's child
Hath not thy Saviour been too much revil'd . . ..
("An address to the Deist—1767"; see appendix for complete version of this hitherto unpublished poem)

Also in her patriotic poems there is racial identification:

New England first a wilderness was found
Till for a continent 'twas destin'd round
From feild [sic] to feild [sic] the savage monster run
E'r yet Brittania had her work begun
Thy Power, O Liberty, makes strong the weak
And (wond'rous instinct) Ethiopians speak
("America")

In "To Maecenas," the first poem in her 1773 volume, she is everywhere deferential and quite personal:

Not you, my friend, these plaintive strains become,
Not you, whose bosom is the *Muses* home;
When they from tow'ring *Helicon* retire,
They fan in you the bright immortal fire,
But I less happy, cannot raise the song,
The fault'ring music dies upon my tongue.
The happier *Terence* all the choir inspir'd,
His soul replenish'd, and his bosom fir'd;

But say, ye *Muses*, why this partial grace,
To one alone of *Afric's* sable race;
From age to age transmitting thus his name
With the first glory in the rolls of fame?

Terence was an African by birth. Throughout the poem, Phillis thanks Maecenas (likely John Wheatley, her benevolent master) and wonders why the ancient Muses saw fit to honor only Terence, a single representative of the African race.

Phillis could be more overt in her acknowledgements of and concern for her fellow Blacks. In the *Royal American Magazine* for December, 1774, she published a poem, "To a Gentleman of the Navy," and there was also published in the same issue, the naval gentleman's reply, a poem titled "The Answer." In "The Answer," the anonymous officer waxed extreme in his praise of Africa and Phillis. In January, 1775, in the same magazine, Phillis acknowledged the naval gentleman's poem by publishing a work called "Reply." In this "Reply," Phillis becomes poetically laudatory of Africa. Whether she was stirred by the officer's versified reminisence of his prospect of Africa and Africans into autobiographical recollections, or whether she was simply trying to match his uncommon praise of Africa, is not known. What is clear is that herein Phillis Wheatley's praise of Africa is pioneering in the Black American literary tradition.

. . . In fair description are thy powers display'd
In artless grottos, and the sylvan shade;
Charm'd with thy painting, how my bosom burns!
And pleasing Gambia on my soul returns,
With native grace in spring's luxuriant reign,
Smiles the gay mead, and Eden blooms again,
The various bower, the tuneful flowing stream,
The soft retreats, the lovers golden dream,
Her soul spontaneous, yields exhaustless stores;
For phoebus revels on her verdant shores.
Whose flowery births, a fragrant train appear,
And crown the youth throughout the smiling year,
    There, as in Britain's favour'd isle, behold
The bending harvest ripen into gold!

Just as thy views of Afric's blissful plain,
On the warm limits of the land and main.
Pleas'd with the theme, see sportive fancy play,
In realms devoted to the God of day!

Such poetic praise of Africa was not written by many other American Blacks until the Harlem Renaissance. In supposed contrast is the poem, "On Being Brought From Africa to America" (1773), in which many of her critics see Phillis' embarrassed, defensive feelings about her African homeland:

'Twas mercy brought me from my *Pagan* land,
Taught my benighted soul to understand
That there's a God, that there's a *Saviour* too:
Once I redemption neither sought nor knew.
Some view our sable race with scornful eye,
"There colour is a diabolic die."
Remember, *Christians, Negroes,* black as *Cain,*
May be refin'd, and join th'angelic train.

Many interpret this poem to mean that, ingratiatingly, fawningly, Phillis is arguing for recognition of racial and human similarities between Black and whites, that "*Negroes,* black as *Cain,*" may be just as good as white folks, even though they are black. But Phillis knew colonial racism, knew she was Black, yet, as is clear from the sincerity of her earliest poems in 1767, six years after she landed in America, knew that what mattered more than being African or American, male or female, Loyalist or Patriot, was being a Christian. So this poem could easily be regarded as the first poetic protest in Black American literature to assert that, think and claim what white "Christians" will, there is not and never will be any Biblical color barrier to anyone becoming a Christian.

Another poem given over entirely to a Black is "To S.M., a Young African Painter, on Seeing His Works" (1773). "S.M." has already been identified as "Scipio Moorhead, and it has also been noted that only in the title of the poem does Phillis indicate his race. Again, however, as with "On Being Brought From Africa to America," she is more concerned with piety than with Blackness; her admiration for Moorhead is evident enough without rhetorical elaboration of his Blackness:

To show the lab'ring bosom's deep intent,
And thought in living characters to paint,
When first thy pencil did those beauties give,
And breathing figures learnt from thee to live,
How did those prospects give my soul delight,
A new creation rushing on my sight?
Still, wond'rous youth! each noble path pursue,
On deathless glories fix thine ardent view:
Still may the painter's and the poet's fire
To aid thy pencil, and thy verse conspire!
And may the charms of each seraphic theme
Conduct thy footsteps to immortal fame! . . . .
High to the blissful wonders of the skies
Elate thy soul, and raise thy wishful eyes.
Thrice happy, when exalted to survey
That splendid city, crown'd with endless day . . .

And if, in another poem written about and for a fellow Black, Phillis is sparing in racial identifications, she is no less sincere in her zeal for his apparent orthodox ways:

While hireling scribbers prostitue their pen,
Creating virtues for abandoned men,
Ascribing merit to the vicious great,
And basely flatter whom they ought to hate—
Be mine the just, the grateful task to scan
Tho'effulgent virtues of a *sable* man:
Trace the good action to the source sublime
And mark its progress to the death of time.
Alternate seasons quickly pass away,
And the *sixth* lustre crowns this natal day
Since first my Pompey, humble, modest, wise,
Shot the bright dawn of reason from his eyes:
Nor was his morn o'ercast by folly's cloud;
Ne'er pressed his footsteps 'mong the giddy crowd:
Even the gay season of luxuriant youth
Was wisely spent to ascertain the truth.
Religious precepts formed his darling plan,
And virtue's dictates stamped him *real* man—
Long may Pompey live, long live to prove
The sweets of virtue, and the joys of love;
And when these happy annual feats are past,
That day be happiest which will be his last;

Then may his soul triumphantly ascend,
Where *perfect bliss* shall never know an end.
("An Ode/On the Birthday of Pompey Stockridge")

Hopefully, it is clear by now that while she may never have written militantly anti-slavery poetry (for reasons already suggested), Phillis Wheatley (Peters) nevertheless managed to make it known that she was proudly Black and that she was concerned for her fellow Afro-Americans, especially with their Christian identification. But her already demonstrated compassion for her Black peers is even more emphasized in her letters, which, unlike her poems, were not designed for the white reading public, and which are, therefore, more indicative of her genuine racial feelings.

Phillis' prose output comprises some 18 known letters (including covering letters for enclosed poems, and prefatory "notes" to poems), and her 1779 "Proposals" for a projected but never published second volume. Covering 1765-1779, the letters are addressed to a variety of personages: a converted Mohegan Indian, Samson Occom (1723?-1792), while he was lecturing throughout England to raise monies for what has since become Darmouth College in New Hampshire; the Countess of Huntingdon in London and Wales; the Reverend Samuel Hopkins (1721-1803), early abolitionist of Newport, Rhode Island; General George Washington at his Cambridge headquarters; the Earl of Dartmouth in London; Obour (Arbour) Tanner, her lifelonge Black fellow servant friend in Newport. In almost all of these letters Phillis refutes her critics who charge that she was insensitive to the feelings, welfare and aspirations of other Blacks. Again and again, Phillis writes of her deep concern for Blacks, and even of her cooperation in helping to fund what was likely the first Black American back-to-Africa attempt.

Her first letter to the Reverend Samson Occom does not seem to be extant. It is only referred to in a short letter written by John Wheatley, her master, to the publisher of her 1773 volume. Supplying a helpful paragraph of biographical details, the letter goes on:

> . . . As to her writing, her own curiosity led her/to it; and this she learnt in so short a Time, that in/the Year 1765, she wrote a letter to the Rev./Mr. Occom, the *Indian* Minister, while in *England.*/ . . .

Another letter, written by Phillis in England to Occom in Boston, "in the summer of 1773," is also only referred to.[80] But there was printed on March 24, 1774, in *The Massachusetts Spy,* a third letter, which she wrote to Occom on February 11. Published in at least two other New England newspapers (March 21, 1774, *Boston Post Boy,* p. 3; March 26, 1774, *The Providence* (R.I.) *Gazette,* p. 2) this letter, genuinely genteel, superficially restrained, is the most subtly biting piece of Black protest Phillis Wheatley ever published. It stands as a documented testimony of her racial awareness and concern. Brilliantly analogyzing Biblical Israelites and her contemporary Blacks, Biblical Egyptians and her contemporary white racists, she points out that every day long-maligned Africa was demonstrating the values of "glorious

> dispensation of civil and/religious liberty, which are so inseparably unit-/ed, that there is little or no enjoyment of one/without the other: Otherwise, perhaps the/Israelites had been less solicitous for their free-/dom from Egyptian Slavery; I do not say they/would have been contented without it, by no/means, for in every human breast, God has im-/planted a principle, which we call love of free-/dom; it is impatient of oppression, and pants/for deliverance—, and by the leave of our modern/ Egyptians I will assert that the same principle/lives in us. God grant deliverance in his own/way and time and get him honour upon all/those whose avarice impels them to countenance/and help forward the calamities of their fellow/creatures. This I desire not for their hurt, but/to convince them of the strange absurdity of their/conduct whose words and actions are so/ diametrically opposite. How well the cry for/liberty, and the reverse disposition, for the exer-/cise of oppressive power over others agree-/I humbly think it does not require the penetra- /tion of a philosopher to determine.

In three newly unearthed and published letters written to the Countess of Huntingdon, Phillis reveals some of the means by which she determinedly would achieve recognition, as well as her abiding concern for Blacks making their mark in the world. The first letter dated "Boston Octr. 25th 1770," is essentially a covering letter for her poem eulogizing the death of the Reverend George Whitefield, chaplain to the Countess. The second, dated "London/June 27, 1773," was written after her trip from Boston to London, "after a fine passage of 5 weeks in the ship London with my young master (advised by my physicians for my Health)." It registers her disappointment at not finding the Countess waiting in her London home, but in Wales, thanks the Countess for allowing Phillis to dedicate the volume to her, and adds other amenities The third, dated "London July 17/1773," notes her grief at being obliged, by news of the grave sickness of Mrs. Wheatley back in Boston, to leave London without seeing the Countess, still in Wales involved, as always, with her promotion of the new Methodism.

> Madam
> I rec'd with mixed sensations of pleasure & disappointment [sic] your Ladiship's message favored by Mr. Rien acquainting us with your pleasure that my Master & I should wait upon you in So. Wales, delighted with your Ladiship [sic] Condescention [sic] to me so unworthy of it. Am sorry to acquaint your Ladiship that the Ship is certainly to Sail next Thursday [on] which I must return to America. I long to see my Friend there, [I am] extremely reluctant to go without having first seen your Ladiship. *It gives me very great satisfaction to hear of an African so worth* [sic] *to be honored with your Ladiship's approbation & Friendship as him whom you call your Brother.* . . . (italics mine)[81]

The "African" referred to by the Countess as "brother" might have been almost any one of several prominent religious Black figures of the times. There was James Albert Ukasaw Gronniosaw, born about 1710, who in his native Guinea, as grandson to a King, costumed himself routinely in gold. But after several enslavements and subsequent poverty in western Europe, he dictated his life story, *A Narrative of the Most Remarkable Particulars in the Life of James Albert Ukasaw Gronniosaw, an African* (1774). Assisted by the Countess, he dedicated the book to her. The "African" called "brother" might refer to Olaudah Equiano, popularly known as Gustavas Vasa, who, born in 1745 in Nigeria, and, like Gronniosaw, kidnapped into slavery as a child, worked his way to freedom and later campaigned on behalf of Christian motivated anti-slavery agitation. Vasa also wrote a narrative of his life, in 2 volumes (London, 1789), and included the Countess among his subscribers. John Marrant, a Black American born in 1755, is another possibility as the "African," in Phillis' letter. Living what he later was mortified to recall as a debauched teen-age life, drinking and whoring and playing the fiddle and the French horn at all night balls and dances, Marrant was confessedly traumatized into strict religious ways when he heard the Reverend George Whitefield preaching in Charlestown, South Carolina. He became eccentric, loathing civilization, crawling about on all fours "like a horse," as he chewed grass for his meals ("and I thought it the best meal I had ever had in my life,") and deliberately drank muddied water, "which some wild pigs had just left.[82] He preached to and converted Nova Scotia Indians, and delivered a sermon in 1784 to Prince Hall's group who later made up the African Masonic Lodge No. 459 and accepted Marrant as chaplain-member. As a preacher he may have been assisted by the Countess, to whose Methodist Connexion he belonged, and who wrote him correspondence in 1786, now extant.

The most probable "African" referred to in the letter is a Philip Quaque (1741-1816). Born on the Gold Coast (now Ghana), Quaque was schooled in England and in 1765 became the first African ordained as a priest in the Church of England. He returned to Africa and, in unanswered letters to England, documented a lifetime of English Christian neglect and African frustration as he failed to bring what he considered adequate Christian education to his people. Further evidence to support the likelihood that the "African . . . Brother" was Quaque derives from the observation that Phillis refers to him in two later letters. The first one follows:

To the Rev. Mr. Samuel Hopkins, of New Port
Rhode Island
BOSTON, Feb. 9, 1774

Rev'd Sir, — I take with pleasure the opportunity by Post, to acquaint you with the arrival of my books from London. I have sealed up a package containing 17 for you, and 2 for Mr. Tanner, and one for Mrs. Mason, and only wait for you to appoint some proper person, by whom I may convey them to you. I received some time ago 20s sterling upon them, by the hands of your son, in a letter from Abour Tanner. *I received at the same time a paper, by which I understand there are two negro* [sic] *men, who are desirous of returning to their native country, to preach the Gospel;* but being much indisposed by the return of my asthmatic complaint, besides the sickness of my mistress, who has been long confined to her bed, and is not expected to live a great while; all these things render it impracticable for me to do anything at present with regard to that paper, *but what I can do in influencing my Christian friends and acquaintances, to promote this laudable design, shall not be wanting.* Methinks, Rev. Sir, this is the beginning of that happy period foretold by the Prophets, when all shall know the Lord from the least to the greatest, and that without the assistance of human Art or Eloquence. My heart expands with sympathetic joy to see at distant time the thick cloud of ignorance dispersing from the face of my benighted country. Europe and America have long been fed with the heavenly provision, and I fear they loath it, while Africa is perishing with a spiritual Famine. O that they could partake of the crumbs, the precious crumbs which fall from the table of these distinquished children of the kingdom.

Their minds are unprejudiced against the truth, therefore 'tis to be hoped they could receive it with their whole hearts I hope that which the divine royal Psalmist says, by inspiration is now on the point of being accomplished, namely, Ethiopia shall soon stretch forth her hands unto God. Of this, Abour Tanner, and I trust many others within your knowledge, are living witnesses. Please to give my love to her, and I intend to write her soon. My best respects attend every kind inquiry after your obliged Humble servant,

PHILLIS WHEATLEY[83]
(italics mine)

The second letter, mentioning Philip Quaque by name, again shows the poet's concern about his attempts to offer Christian education to the sons of fellow Africans:

> *Rev'd Sir*
>
> I received your kind letter last Evening by Mr. Pemberton, by whom also this is to be handed you. I have also rec'd. the Money for the 5 books I sent Obour, & 2/6 more for another. She has wrote me, but the date is 29 April. I am very sorry to hear, that Philip Quaque has made very little or no *apparent* Success in his mission. Yet, I wish that what you hear respecting him, may be only a misinterpretation. Let us not be discouraged, but still hope, that God will bring about his great work, tho' Philip may *not* be the instrument in the Divine Hand to perform this work of wonder, turning the African "*from darkness to light.*" Possibly, if Philip would introduce himself properly to them, (I don't know the reverse) he might be more Successful, and in setting a good example which is more powerfully winning than Instruction. I observe your Reference to the Maps of Guinea, Salmon's Gazetteer, and shall consult them. I have rec'd. in some of the last ships from London 300 more copies of my poems. If you know of any being wanted I flatter myself you will be pleas'd to let me know it, which will be adding one to the many Obligations already confer'd on her, who is, with a due Sense of your kindness,
>
> Your most humble
> And Obedient servant
> PHILLIS WHEATLEY

Boston[84]
May 6, 1774

In both of these letters to Hopkins, it can be plainly seen that Phillis Wheatley was very much concerned about the welfare of her fellow Blacks in America and in Africa. Noticeable also, in these and other letters written by her, is Phillis' practical and continual concern for the sales of her volumes of poems. She may or may not have known that Hopkins was on record as one who did not like poetry, but she certainly was aware that, as a leader of an ambitious missionary-colonization plan, Hopkins needed all of the prominent Black help he could get. Very much an alert woman of her times, she was familiar with the various necessities of Black survival in a racist world.

Most of her known extant letters are directed to Obour Tanner and date from 1772 to 1779. These seven letters are general, personal (although not intimate), and they discuss such matters as recurring bouts of her troublesome asthma, solicitation for sales of her volumes of poems, her mistress, the Revolutionary War and, predictably enough, pious and sincere sympathy for her fellow Blacks. Indeed, the earliest extant letter to Obour is mostly about just this matter of the advent of Christianity for Blacks:

To Arbour Tanner, in Newport.

BOSTON May 19th 1772

DEAR SISTER,—I rec'd your favour of February 6th for which I give you my sincere thanks. I greatly rejoice with you in that realizing view, and I hope experience of the saving change which you so emphatically describe. Happy were it for us if we could arrive to that evangelical Repentance, and the true holiness of the heart which you mention. Inexpressibly happy should we be could we have a due sense of the beauties and excellence of the crucified Saviour. In his Crucifixion may be seen marvellous displays of Grace and Love, sufficient to draw and invite us to the rich and endless treasures of his mercy; let us rejoice in and adore the wonders of God's infinite Love in bringing us from a land semblant of darkness itself, and where the divine light of revelation (being obscur'd) is as darkness. Here the knowledge of the true God and eternal life are made manifest; but there, profound ignorance overshadows the land. Your observation is true, namely, that there was nothing in us to recommend us to God. Many of our fellow creatures are pass'd by, when the bowels of divine love expanded toward us. May this goodness & long suffering of God lead us to unfeign'd repentance.

It gives me very great pleasure to hear of so many of my nation, seeking with eagerness the way of true felicity. O may we all meet at length in that happy mansion. I hope the correspondence between us will continue, (my being much indispos'd this winter past, was the reason of my not answering yours before now) which correspondence I hope may have the happy effect of improving our mutual friendship. Till we meet in the regions of consummate blessedness, let us endeavor by the assistance of divine grace, to live the life, and we shall die the death of the Righteous. May this be our happy case, and of those who are travelling to the region of Felicity, is the earnest request of your affectionate

Friend & humble servant PHILLIS WHEATLEY[85]

It is important to remember that here, as in her poem "On Being Brought From Africa to America," Phillis is not necessarily asserting that Africans are backward, or in error, because they are Africans; they are wrong and suffering because they are not Christians.

After the death of Mrs. Susanna Wheatley on March 3, 1774, Phillis soon understood that she was largely on her own in a merciless competitively and crude land. If she took an apartment by herself, as some feel she did, it is all the more understandable that her subsequent letters emphasize concern for the sale of her books, for monies from such sales represented her subsistence. On May 6, while still in grievous mourning, she manages to include, in a letter to Obour, mention of the sales of her poetry: "I have rec'd the money you sent for the 5 books & 2/6 more for another, which I now send & wish safe to hand. Your tenderness for my welfare demands my gratitude . . . I have rec'd by some of the last ships 300 more of my poems." Likely obliged to redouble her efforts to sell her poems for her livelihood, Phillis may have carried her volumes from door to door, and she may even have read selections of her poems to potential lady customers. On September 19, 1774, a prominent white woman, Deborah Cushing, wrote to her equally prominent husband a letter which may explain Phillis' sales techniques (the text is unedited):

> I rote you/by Mr. Cary and sent you one of Phillis Wheatleys books/which you will wonder att by Mrs. Dickerson and Miss Clymer Mrs. Bull with some other Ladys ware so pleased with Phillis and her performances that they bought her Books/ and got her to compose peices for them which put/me in mind of Ms Vanhorn to hume I thought it would/be very agreeabel I am obligged[86]

The "peices" Phillis composed for the pleasure of these ladies have not yet been identified, but if being "pleased with Phillis and her performances" meant that Phillis did read her poems before the assembled ladies, then Phillis was unusually active on her own behalf in trying to survive.

After being obliged, with thousands of others, to retreat from Boston during the seige of 1775-1776, she very probably found temporary refuge with her old friend and tutor, Mary Wheatley (Lathrop), whose husband, the Reverend John Lathrop, retired to Providence, Rhode Island, during this year. It is in this year also that Phillis composed one of her more famous patriotic poems with a covering letter dated and addressed, "Providence, Oct. 26, 1775./His Excellency Gen. Washington." The widely anthologized poem is entitled "To His Excellency General Washington," and contains the name "Columbia" to poetically identify America. Many readers believe that she was the first American poet to use that name for America, but there is documented evidence that American poets used that term as early as 1761[87] General Washington acknowledged the tributary piece, in a letter to her dated "Cambridge, February 28, 1776," in which he invited Phillis to visit him at his headquarters: "If you should ever come to Cambridge or near head-quarters, I shall be happy to see a person so favored by the Muses, and to whom nature has been so liberal and beneficent in her dispensations." Phillis was received by Washington for an interesting and courteous half hour at his headquarters.

For some years after the date of her Washington poem, it is not known exactly what Phillis did or where she lived. If she had been enjoying assistance from John Wheatley, her former master, it ended on March 12, 1778, when he died. Nathaniel Wheatley, her escort on the Boston to London 1773 trip, decided to live in England, and Mary Wheatley Lathrop passed on in September of 1778. For the first time in her protected life, Phillis Wheatley found herself without the help of the friends who had reared and educated her. Phillis then seems to have moved, for it is recorded that, as "free Negroes," Phillis Wheatley and John Peters married on April 1, 1778. In a letter headed "Bost-ton, May 29th '78," Phillis wrote to Obour Tanner (who was now with "her folks" in Worcester, Massachusetts) and included the name and address of her husband:

Miss Obour Tanner, Worcester.
DEAR OBOUR, — I am exceedingly glad to hear from you by Mrs. Tanner, and wish you had timely notice of her departure, so as to have wrote me; next to that is the pleasure of hearing you are well. The vast variety of scenes that have pass'd before us these 3 years past, will to a reasonable mind serve to convince us of the uncertain duration of all things temporal, and the proper result of such a consideration is an ardent desire of a preparation for, a state and enjoyments which are more suitable to the immortal mind. You will do me a great favour if you'll write me by every opportunity. Direct your letters under cover to Mr. John Peters in Queen Street. I have but half an hour's notice; and must apologize for this hasty scrawl. I am most affectionately, My dear Obour, your sincere friend

PHILLIS WHEATLEY[88]

In this letter, although married for a month, Phillis seems restrained about her personal life, and does not even use her married name. She does not yet indicate that her marriage, as reported, was not the best. In a later letter, written from Boston and dated "May 10, 1779," a year after she was married, Phillis seems nervous and terse. She does use her married name, but all does not seem domestically tranquil:

Dr. Obour, — By this opportunity I have the pleasure to inform you that I am well and hope you are so; tho' I have been silent, I have not been unmindful of you, but a variety of hindrances was the cause of my not writing to you. But in time to come I hope our correspondence will revive—and revive in better times—pray write me soon, for I long to hear from you—you may depend on constant replies—I wish you much happiness, and am

Dr. Obour, your friend and sister

PHILLIS PETERS[89]

Whether or not their correspondence did continue is not known, for this is the last dated of the presently extant letters from Phillis Wheatley to Obour Tanner. It is not likely that there was much, if any, correspondence after this date, for, if reports of Phillis' last years in poverty and wretchedness and utter neglect as a common domestic in a boarding house are true, there was now no time for anything but consideration of survival. Throughout her literary career Phillis had depended largely on the sales of her poems, gaining a reputation that she probably tried to exploit again in behalf of her family, which included a husband who was difficult, to say the least. Her Proposals for a second volume of poems and letters, printed in the *Evening Post and General Advertiser* for October 30, 1779, projected a *"volume of Poems & Letters on various subjects, dedicated to the Right Hon. Benjamin Franklin Esq: One of the Ambassadors of the United States at the Court of France."* It failed to interest enough subscribers, and the volume was never published.

Regrettably, we do not have an original or copy of a single letter written by Obour Tanner to Phillis. Nor do we have letters, or copies, written to Phillis from most of her other known correspondents: the Countess of Huntingdon, the Reverend Samson Occom, the Reverend Samuel Hopkins. Almost discarded, the letter written to her from General Washington was published fifty years after her death. It is known that she corresponded with an unidentified "English Gentleman" who she met during her London visit,[90] but no letters have yet been traced. Although she also corresponded, for years, with Thomas Wallcut (1758-1840) a Wheatley relative and a close friend, only one inconsequential note from Wallcut to her in extant. (See appendix) Also extant is a note written to her by Captain John Paul Jones, famous American naval hero.[91] Such letters would add immeasurably, of course, to the still incomplete portrait of a most unusual Black woman of colonial America.

When properly read, in the context of her times, the available data—poems, letters, a memoir, accounts of the times—go far toward documenting the engaging story of how she encountered and dealt with various obstacles to her finding and asserting her Black and poetic worth. There is indeed evidence enough to sustain the belief that Phillis Wheatley did survive those raw Black American beginnings to endure as Christian, as woman, and as Black

American poet. Phillis Wheatley not only belongs squarely in the Black American literary tradition; she, almost single-handedly, succeeded in creating that tradition.

Appendices

NEWLY PUBLISHED POEMS
by PHILLIS WHEATLEY

(Note: It is not quite correct to regard all four of the following poems as "new" in the strictest sense of that word, for the first three are simply early versions of poems. The first poem, "A Poem on the Death of Charles Eliot, aged 12 months," was revised and published as "A Funeral Poem on the Death of C.E. An Infant of Twelve Months" in her 1773 volume. The next two poems are manuscript versions of a poem that has a total of five versions: two appear in Robert C. Kuncio's article (q.v.), and another version appears in Lorenzo Greene's *The Negro in Colonial New England* (New York, 1942), p. 245. The fourth poem "An address to the Deist—1767," is a newly discovered poem, and is published here from a manuscript located in the Massachusetts Historical Society. The appearance of these early versions of poems will prove helpful to Wheatley readers concerned with her patterned revisions.)

A

A Poem on the Death of Charles Eliot,
aged 12 months

Thro' airy realms, he wings his infant flight,
To purer regions of celestial light,
Unmov'd he sees uncumber'd systems roll
Beneath his feet, the universal whole
In just succession run their destin'd round
And circling wonders spread the dread profound;
Th'etheral now, and now the starry skies,
With glowing splendors strike his wand'ring eyes.
The heav'nly legions, views with joy unknown,
Press his soft hand, and seat him on the throne,
And smiling thus: "To this divine abode,
"The Seat of Saints, of Angels, and of God:
"Thrice welcome hero."—The raptur'd babe replies,
"Thanks to my God, who snatch'd me to the skies,
"Ere vice triumphant had possess'd my heart;
"Ere yet the tempter claim'd my better part;

"Ere yet I knew temptation's dread intent;
"Ere yet on Sin's most deadly actions bent;
"Ere yet the road for horrid crimes I know,
"Not rais'd with vanity, or oppress'd with wo;
"But soon arriv'd to heaven's bright port assign'd.
"Now glories rush on my expanding mind;
"A noble ardor now, my bosom fires,
"To utter what the heav'nly muse inspires;"
Joyful he spoke—exulting cherubs round
Clap loud their pinions, and the plains resound.
Say parents! why this unavailing moan?
Why heave your bosoms with the rising groan?
To Charles, the happy subject of my song,
A happier world, and noble strains belong.
Say, would you tear him from the realms above,
Or make less happy, frantic in your love?
Doth his beatitude increase your pain,
Or could you welcome to this earth again
The Son of bliss? — No, with Superior air,
Methinks he answers with a smile severe,
"Thrones and dominions cannot tempt me there."
But still you cry, "O Charles! thy manly mind,
"Enwraps our souls and all thy actions blind;
"Our only hope, more dear than vital breath,
"Twelve months resolv'd and sunk in shades of death!
"Engaging infant! Nightly visions give
"Thee to our arms, and we with joy receive;
"We fain would clasp the phantom to our breast,
"The phantom flies, and leaves the soul unblest!"
Prepare to meet your dearest infant friend
While joys are pure and glory's without end.

Phillis Wheatley

Boston, Sept. 1st 1772

An address to the Atheist, by P. Wheatley at the age of 14 years—1767

Muse! where shall I begin this spacious feild [sic]
To tell what curses unbeleif [sic] doth yield?
Thou who dost daily feel his hand and rod
Darest thou deny the essence of a God!
If there's no heav'n, ah! wither wilt thou go
Make thy Ilysium in the Shade below?
If there's no God from whom did all things Spring
He made the *greatest* and *minutest* thing
Angelic ranks no less his Power Display
Than the least mite scarce to Day

With vast astonishment my soul is struck
Have Reason's powers thy darken'd breast forsook?
The Laws deep Graven by the hand of God,
Seal'd with Immanuel's all-redeeming blood:
This second point thy folly dares deny
On thy devoted head for vengeance cry
Turn then I pray thee from the dangerous road
Rise from the dust and seek the mighty God,
His is bright truth without a dark disguise
And his are wisdom's all beholding Eyes:
With labour'd snares our adversary great
Witholds from us the kingdom and the Seat
Bliss weeping waits thee in her arms to fly
To her own regions of felicity
Perhaps thy ignorance will ask us where?
To the *Corner stone* he will declare.
Thy heart is unbeleif [sic] will harden'd grow
Tho' much indulged in vicious pleasure now
Thou tak'st usual means; the paths forbear
Unkind to others to thy self severe
Methinks I see the consequence thou'rt blind
Thy unbeleif [sic] disturbs the Peaceful Mind
The endless scene too far for me to tread
Too great to utter from so weak a head.
That Man his maker's love divine might know
In heaven's high formament he placed his Bow
To show his covenant for ever sure
To endless Ahe unchanging to endure
He made the Heavens and earth, that lasting Spring
Of Admiration! To whom dost thou bring
Thy grateful tribute? Adoration pay
To heathen Gods? Can wise *Apollo* say
Tis I that saves thee from the deepest hell,
Minerva teach thee all thy days to tell?
Doth Pluto tell thee thou shalt see the shade
Of fell perdition for transgressions made?
Doth Cupid in thy breast that warmth inspire
To love thy Brother, which is God's desire?
Atheist! behold the wide extend'd skys
And wisdom infinite shall strike thine eyes
Mark rising Sol when far he spread his Ray
And his Commission read "To rule the Day"
At night behold that Silver Regent bright
And her command to lead the train of night
Lo! how the stars all vocal in his praise
Witness his essence in celestial lays!

Atheism Boston, July 1769

Where now shall I begin this Spacious feild [sic]
To tell what curses unbeleif [sic] doth yield
Thou that dost daily feel his hand and rod
And dare deny the essence of a God
If there's no heaven whither wilt thou go?
Make thy elysium in the shade below
If there's no God from whence did all things Spring
He made the greatest and minutest thing
With great astonishment my Soul is struck
O rashness great, hast thou thy sense forsook
Hast thou forgot the preterperfect days
They are recorded in the book of praise
If twas not written by the hand of God
Why was it sealed with Immanuels blood
Tho 'tis a second point thou dost deny,
Unmeasur'd vengence [sic] Scarlet sins do cry
Now turn I pray thee from the dangerous road
Rise from the dust and seek the mighty God
By whom great mercy we do move and live
Whose loving kindness doth our sins forgive
'Tis beelzebub our adversary great
Withholds from us the kingdom and the seat
Bliss weeping waits us in her arms to fly
To the vast regions of Felicity
Perhaps thy Ignorance will ask us where
Go to the corner stone, it will declare
Thy heart in unbeleif [sic] will harder grow
Altho' thou Dost it for pleasure now
Methinks I see the consequence thou'rt blind
Thy unbeleif [sic] disturbs the peaceful mind
The endless scene too far for me to tread
Too great, to accomplish from so weak a head
If men such wise inventions then should know
In the high firmament who made the bow
That covenant was made for to endure
Made to establish lasting to endure
He made the heavens and earth a lasting Spring
Of admiration; to whom dost thou bring
Thy thanks and tribute, adoration pay
To heathen Gods? can wise Apollo say
Tis I that saves from the lowest Hell
Minerva teach thee all thy Days to tell
Doth Pluto tell thee thou shalt see the shade
Of fell perdition for thy learning made
Doth Cupid in thy breast that warmth inspire

To love thy brother, which is gods desire
Look thou above and see who made the sky
Nothing more lucied to an atheists eye
Look thou beneath and see each purling stream
It surely cannot a delusion seem
Mark rising Pheobus [sic] when he spreads his ray
And his Commission for to guide the day
All night keep watch and see a Cynthia bright
And her commission for to guide the night
See how the stars when thy do sing his praise
Witness his essence in celestial lays

An address to the Deist—1767

Must Ethiopians be employ'd for you?
Much I rejoice if any good I do.
I ask O unbeliever, Satan's child
Hath not thy Saviour been too much revil'd
Th' auspicious rays that round his temples shine
Do still declare him to be Christ divine
Doth not the great *Eternal* call him Son
Is he not pleased with his beloved One?
How canst thou thus divide the Trinity—
The blest the Holy the eternal three
Tis Satan's snares are fluttering in the wind
Whereby he doth ensare the foolish mind
God, the Eternal orders this to be
Sees thy vain arguments to divide the three
Can'st thou not see the Consequence in store?
Begin th' Almighty monarch to adore
Attend to Reason whispering in thine ear
Seek the Eternal while he is so near
Full in thy view I point each path I know
Lest to the vale of black dispair [sic] I go
At the last day where wilt thou hide thy face
That day approaching is no time for Grace
Too late percieve [sic] thyself undone and lost
Too late own Father, Son, and Holy Ghost.
Who trod the wine-press of Jehovah's wrath?
Who brought us prayer and promis'd grace and faith?
Who but the Son, who reigns supremely blest
Ever, and ever, in immortal rest?
The vilest prodigal who comes to God
Is not cast out but bro't by Jesus' blood
When to the faithless Jews he oft did cry
Some own'd this teacher some made him a lie

He came to you in mean apparel clad
He came to save us from our sins and had
Compassion more than language can express.
Pains his companions, and his friends distress
Immanuel on the cross those pains did bear
Will the eternal our petitions hear?
Ah! wond'rous Destiny his life he said
"Father forgive them," thus the Saviour pray'd
Nail'd was King Jesus on the cross for us
For our transgressions he sustained the Curse.

B

Found between the pages of *The/Interesting Narrative/of/the Life/of/Olaudah Equiano/or/Gustavus Vassa,/the African/Written by Himself/ . . . To Which are added/Poems on Various Subjects, by/Phillis Wheatley* (sic)/*Negro Servant to Mr. John Wheatley* (sic) *of Boston in New England* (Halifax, 1814), the following manuscript poem is untitled, undated and unsigned, but the ingenuous sentiments and, more importantly, the handwriting very much resemble Phillis'.

How vain are all things here below
How false and yet how fair
Each pleasure hath its poison too
And every sweet a snare

The brightest things below the sky
Give but a flattering light
We should suspect some danger nigh
Where we *posses* delight—

Oud dearest joys, and nearest friends
The partners of our blood
How they divide our wavering mind
And leave *but half* for God.

Dear Saviour, let thy beauties be
My soul's eternal food:
And grace command my heart away
From all created good.

C

Letter from Thomas Wallcut to Phillis Wheatley

Nov 17 1774

Canada Montreal
Much Esteem'd Madam

According to your Design and my promise of Writing I now (comply?) . . . Not without Reluctance the you Excuse me with only Giving you 2 or three lines as what I write will hardly bear reading much more criticizing but I have just thought that you said you don't like Apologies therefore Desist. However I hope you will [so] good as not to expose it but if any body shall read this letter beside yourself Perhaps they [would?] say why I should think that one who is in another country and nation would find matter of subject or the contrast for a letter to such a one I would reply that Everyone has not the gift of letter Writing

To Miss Phillis Wheatley*

but I beg that no one may have the advantage but yourself—I believe you are by this time tired of Reading such Nonsense therefore with being remembered to all your Dear family I subscribe my best

Your sincere & oblig'd friend
Thomas Wallcut

Please to indulge me with an answer and that will Convince me that you have not got out of conceit of me . . .

*Written, in Wallcut's hand, at the bottom of page 1 of this letter of two pages

FOOTNOTES

1. Benjamin Brawley, *The Negro in Literature and Art* (New York, 1918), p. 161.
2. Charoltte Wright, *The Poems of Phillis Wheatley* (Philadelphia, 1930), p. v.
3. Margarette Matilda Odell, Geo. W. Light, "Memoir" in *Memoir and Poems of Phillis Wheatley* (Boston, 1834), p. 28; hereinafter referred to as "Memoir."
4. *Ibid.,* p. 28.
5. Nathaniel Shurtleff, "Phillis Wheatley, the Negro Slave Poet," in *Proceedings of the Massachusetts Historical Society,* VII (1863-64), 9; hereinafter referred to as *Proceedings.*
6. C.J. Straford, "Extracts from the Journal of C.J. Straford, *Proceedings* XIV (1876-77), 290.
7. "Memoir," p. 10.
8. John Wheatley, "Letter," in *Memoir and Poems of Phillis Wheatley* (Boston, 1834), p. 36.
9. "Memoir," p. 11.
10. *Ibid.,* p. 12
11. Wright, p. iv.
12. *Newport* (Rhode Island) *Mercury,* p. 3, column 3; see also Carl Bridenbaugh, "The Earliest Published Poem of Phillis Wheatley," *New England Quarterly,* XLII, No. 4 (December, 1969), 583-584.
13. Sarah D. Jackson, "Letters of Phillis Wheatley and Susanna Wheatley," *Journal of Negro History,* LVII, No. 2 (April, 1972), 212.
14. A common notion is that it was unusual for Blacks to be communicants or members of colonial American churches; but if, among the catalogued members of the Old South Church, single-name entries refer to Blacks as with "Phillis" (Wheatley), then Phillis was not the first or only black member so listed. The first recorded single-name entry in this catalogue of Old South members is a "Maria" listed as a member as of July 7, 1728. Other single-name entries between that date and the August 18, 1771, date of Phillis' membership include: "James," August 20, 1738; "Rose," Sept. 16, 1739; "Scipio" and "Ann," March 1, 1740; "Cornwall," April 26, 1741; "Thomas," July 17, 1742; "Dinah," April 21, 1745; "Julia," Nov. 29, 1747; "Flora," June 16, 1754; "Bristol," March 18, 1756; "Deborah," Aug. 8, 1756; "Newton," Oct. 26, 1760. Old South Church. *The Two Hundred and Fiftieth Anniversary of the Founding of the Old South Church* (Norwood, Mass., 1919), p. 162.
15. Jackson, p. 214.

16. Benjamin Quarles, *The Negro in the American Revolution* (Chapel Hill, 1961), p. 189.
17. "Memoir," p. 18.
18. Jackson, p. 215.
19. *Proceedings,* VII (1863-64), 275.
20. Idem.
21. "Boston Marriages 1752-1809," *Early History of Boston,* Document 101-1902, (Boston, 1902), p. 441.
22. *Proceedings,* VII (1863-64), 276.
23. "Memoir," p. 20.
24. Arthur Schomburg in Charles F. Heartman, *Phillis Wheatley (Peters): Poems and Letters* (New York, 1915), p. 12.
25. "Memoir," p. 22.
26. In Wylie Sypher, *Guinea's Captive Kings: British Anti-Slavery Literature of the XVIIIth Century* (Chapel Hill, 1942), pp. 283-4.
27. *Letters of Phillis Wheatley, the Negro-Slave Poet of Boston* (privately printed, Boston, 1864), p. 6n.
28. "Memoir," p. 23.
29. *Proceedings,* VIII (1864-65), 461-462.
30. "Memoir" pp. 21-22.
31. Nikki Giovanni, "Nikki Rosa," *Black Judgement* (Detroit, 1968), p. 10.
32. "Memoir," p. 29.
33. *Ibid.,* p. 29n.
34. Winthrop Jordan, *White Over Black* (Baltimore, 1969), p. 285.
35. William H. Robinson, Jr., "Phillis Wheatley: Colonial Quandary," *CLA Journal,* IX, No. 1 (September, 1965), 25-38.
36. Benjamin Rush, "An Address . . . Upon Slave Keeping," in Louis Ruchames, ed., *Racial Thought in America* (New York, 1969), pp. 142-3.
37. Cited in Jordan, pp. 283-4.
38. Cited in Robinson, p. 30.
39. Cited in Jordan, p. 285.
40. (Anonymous), *Dreadful Riot on Negro Hill* (New York, 1828), p. 1.
41. *Idem.*
42. Seymour Gross and John E. Hardy, eds., *Images of the Negro in American Literature* (Chicago, 1966), pp. 3-4.
43. Martin Delany, *The Condition, Elevation, Emigration, and Destiny of the Colored Peoples of the United States* (Philadelphia, 1852), pp. 87-8.
44. Ray Billington, ed., *Journal of Charlotte Forten* (New York, 1953), p. 45.
45. Leroi Jones, *Home* (New York, 1966), pp. 105-106.

46. Addison Gayle, "The Function of Black Literature at the Present Time," *Black Aesthetic* (New York, 1971), p. 409.
47. Nathaniel Huggins, *Harlem Renaissance* (New York, 1971), p. 199.
48. Vernon Loggins, *The Negro Author* (New York, 1941), p. 24.
49. "Memoir," p. 10.
50. Melvin H. Buxbaum, "Cyrus Bustill's Address to the Blacks of Philadelphia, 1787," *William and Mary Quarterly*, XXIX, No. 1 (January 1972), 104.
51. Cited in William H. Robinson, ed., *Early Black American Prose* (Dubuque, 1971), pp. 48-9.
52. John Marrant, *A Sermon by the Rev. Bro. Marrant*, (n. p., 1784), p. 14.
53. John Ferguson, *Memoir of the Life and Character of Rev. Samuel Hopkins* (Boston, 1830), pp. 82-3.
54. Edward A. Parks, *Memoir of Life and Character of Samuel Hopkins* (Boston, 1854), p. 117.
55. Carter G. Woodson, ed., *Negro Orations and Their Orators* (Washington, 1925), p. 14.
56. Julian D. Mason, *The Poems of Phillis Wheatley* (Chapel Hill, 1966), p. xxx.
57. Robert C. Kuncio, "Some Unpublished Poems of Phillis Wheatley," *New England Quarterly*, XLIII (June 1970), 288.
58. *Ibid.*, p. 290.
59. *Ibid.*, p. 291.
60. *Ibid.*, p. 290.
61. *Proceedings*, VII (1863-64), 165.
62. Mason, p. 97.
63. *Idem.*
64. *Ibid.*, pp. 73-4.
65. Countee Cullen, ed., *Caroling Dusk* (New York, 1927), p. ix.
66. Kuncio, p. 288n.
67. *Ibid.*
68. Loggins, p. 245.
69. "Memoir," p. 19.
70. Leonard Larabee, ed., *The Papers of Benjamin Franklin*, II (New York, 1969), p. 291.
71. Mason, p. 41n.
72. Anna and Walter Ricketson, *New Bedford of the Past* (Cambridge, 1903), p. 153.
73. Hamilton A. Hill, *A History of the Old South Church* (Cambridge, 1890), p. 90.
74. Lorenzo Greene, *The Negro in Colonial New England* (New York, 1952), p. 324.
75. *Ibid.*, p. 332.

76. Letter from William Barrell to John Andrews, February 24, 1773 (Massachusetts Historical Society).
77. *Idem.*
78. Benjamin Brawley, *Early Negro American Writers* (Chapel Hill, 1935), p. 35.
79. Arthur P. Davis, "Personal Elements in the Poetry of Phillis Wheatley," *Phylon,* XIII (Second Quarter 1953), 192-98.
81. Jackson, p. 215.
82. John Marrant, *A Narrative/of the/Lord's Wonderful Dealing with/John Marrant,/a Black,* Seventh edition (London, 1802), p. 17.
83. Benjamin Quarles, "A Phillis Wheatley Letter," *Journal of Negro History,* XXIV (1949), 463-64.
84. Chamberlain Collection of Letters, A.6.20. Boston Public Library.
85. *Proceedings,* VII (1863-64), 273-74.
86. Letter from Deborah Cushing to her Husband (Cushing Collection of Letters, Massachusetts Historical Society).
87. Albert H. Hoyt, "The Name Columbia," *New England Historical and Genealogical Registry for the Year 1886,* (Boston, 1886), pp. 310-13.
88. *Proceedings,* VII (1863-64), 273-74.
89. *Idem.*
90. Harold Blodgett, *Samson Occom* (Hanover, N. H., 1935) p. 15n.
91. Samuel Eliot Morrison, *John Paul Jones: A Sailor's Biography* (Boston, 1959), pp. 112-113; for a printed copy of Jones' note to Phillis, see Sidney Kaplan, *The Black Presence in the Era of the American Revolution: 1700-1800.* (Connecticut, 1973), p. 162.

A Bibliographical Note

PRE-1773 POEMS AND THEIR REVISIONS

For over 200 years, in Europe and America, Phillis Wheatley's poems have been quoted, analyzed and variously edited in diaries, letters, newspapers, magazines and textbooks. Her bibliography is too vast for an exhaustive display in these few pages. However, a few words might be said about her individually published poems, her collected volume, her letters, and selected memoris of her life, the aim being to focus on recent and new information.

Some of her poems composed before her celebrated volume, *Poems on Various Subjects, Religious and Moral,* have remained in manuscript until recent publication, while other poems, some chosen for inclusion in her 1773 volume, appeared first in broadside and/or manuscript versions, which differ (considerably, in some cases) from their revised appearances in the 1773 collection. Her first published poems was "On Messrs. Hussey and Coffin," a 29-line effort which came out in the December 21, 1767 issue of the Newport (Rhode Island) *Mercury,* a newspaper. It was reprinted by Carl Bridenbaugh in "The Earliest Published Poem of Phillis Wheatley," *New England Quarterly,* XLII (December, 1969), 583-4, and is also published herewith. In June, 1970, Robert C. Kuncio of the Historical Society of Pennsylvania brought out "Some Unpublished Poems of Phillis Wheatley," *New England Quarterly,* XLIII, 287-297, from manuscripts discovered in the Historical Society and in the Library Company of Philadelphia. They were titled "To the King's most excellent Majesty on his repealing the american [sic] Stamp Act"; "On the death of Mr. Snider Murder'd by Richardson"; "America"; "Atheism" (and a contemporary copy of the same poem, titled "On Atheism"); and "To the honorable Commodore Hood on his pardoning a deserter." Kuncio estimates that these undated poems were composed between 1768 and 1770. While neither manuscript version of the poems concerning atheism has any date, two other manuscript versions are dated by Phillis: "An address to the Atheist, by P. Wheatley at the age of 14 years—1767"; and "Atheism, Boston, July 1769." Both manuscripts are in the Massachusetts Historical Society and are published herewith. A fifth version of the same poem appears in Lorenzo J. Greene, *The Negro in Colonial New England:* 1620-1776 (New York, 1942)), p. 245, based on a photostatic copy of a manuscript located in the Library Company of Philadelphia. Helping to fix more firmly the date of the manuscript "To the honorable Commodore Hood on his pardoning a deserter" is the following note found in the February 1769 issue of *The Gentleman's Magazine, and Historical Chronicle* . . . (London), Vol. XXXIX, p. 105: "Boston, New England, Dec. 2. At a court martial aboard the *Mermaid* two sailors were sentenced to be flogged for desertion and one to be hanged; but just as sentence was to be executed upon the latter a reprieve arrived for him from Commodore Hood." Another poem composed about this time is "On Friendship," dated "Boston/July 15, 1769, published in William H. Robinson, *Early Black American Poets* (Dubuque, Iowa, 1969), pp. 111-112. Also published in Robinson, p. 111, is "An Ode/On the Birthday of Pompey Stockbridge," undated and unsigned but regarded as written by Miss Wheatley.

Many of the poems which make up the 1773 collection are revisions of earlier versions. "To the University of Cambridge in New England" (1773) in manuscript form is "To the University of Cambridge, Wrote in 1767." The manuscript, in the American Antiquarian Society, is published in Julian D. Mason, *The Poems of Phillis Wheatley* Chapel Hill, 1966), pp. 63-4. The manuscript "To the King's most excellent Majesty on his repealing the american (sic) Stamp Act" was revised and dated for the 1773 volume as "To the King's Most Excellent Majesty. 1768." "On the Death of the Rev. Dr. Sewell, (sic) 1769" is a revision, for the 1773 volume, of the manuscript "On the Death of the Rev'd Dr. Sewall (sic). 1769," located in the American Antiquarian Society. "On the Death of the Rev. Mr. George Whitefield. 1770," (1773) is one of several versions of this extremely popular and much reprinted poem. Phillis refers to a manuscript version of it (not yet seen) in a covering letter to the Countess of Huntingdon dated "Boston Oct. 25th, 1770." This letter was published by Sarah Dunlap Jackson in "Letters of Phillis Wheatley and Susanna Wheatley," *Journal of Negro History,* LVII, No. 2 (April, 1972), 212. "To Mrs. Leonard on the Death of her Husband," (1771) was a broadside and was revised as "To a Lady on the Death of her Husband" (1773), Dated "Boston, June 16th, 1772," "To the Rev. Mr. Pitkin on the Death of his Lady" is likewise a broadside, located in the Historical Society of Pennsylvania, revised as "To a Clergyman on the Death of his Lady" (1773). "On Recollection" (1773) is a revised version of another popular poem, earlier published in the March 22, 1772 edition of *The London Magazine; Or, Gentleman's Monthly Intelligencer,* Vol. XLI, pp. 134-135; and also in *The Annual Register, or a View of the History, Politics, and Literature for the year 1772,* fifth edition, (London, 1795), pp. 214-15. Revised for the 1773 volume, it was selected and displayed in the September, 1773 issue of *Gentleman's Magazine,* Vol. XLIII (London), with an accompanying publisher's note p. 456, which helps fix the disputed months in which Phillis' volume was published: "This piece is taken from a small collection of Poems on Various Subjects, *just published,* written by Phillis Wheatley, a negro (sic) of Boston. . . . (italics mine). "A Funeral Poem on the Death of C.E. an infant of Twelve Months" (1773) differs in two manuscript versions; one manuscript, "A Poem on the Death of Charles Eliot, aged 12 months. To S. Eliot," is in the Houghton Library of Harvard College, while the other, "A Poem on the Death of Charles Eliot, aged 12 months" (with no dedication to S[amuel] Eliot), dated "Boston, Sept. 1st 1772," is in the Massachusetts Historical Society. And in a letter dated "Boston, N.E. Octo. 10th 1772," Phillis enclosed a manuscript version of a poem which became entitled in her 1773 volume "To the Right Honourable William, Earl of Dartmouth, His

Majesty's Principal Secretary of State for North America, &c," but the manuscript version has not yet been seen.

THE PROPOSAL POEMS

After producing her 1773 collection, Phillis continued to write poems, as is clear from an advertisement in the October 30, 1779 issue of Boston's *Evening Post and General Advertiser,* where Phillis Wheatley's *Proposals,* soliciting advanced subscribers for a projected but never published volume, listed the titles of 33 poems and 13 numbered titles to letters she had written. Along with others, several of these Proposal poems were published during her lifetime. "An Elegy, To Miss Mary Moorhead, on the DEATH of her Father, the Rev. Mr. JOHN MOORHEAD" appeared as a broadside (in Massachusetts Historical Society) dated "Boston, Decm./15 1773"; The *Proposal* title to "To Lieut R— of the Royal Navy" and the next one, "To the same," are likely the poems published as "To a Gentleman of the Navy for the *Royal American Magazine,*" dated "Boston, October 30th, 1774," appearing in *The Royal American Magazine*. I (Dec, 1774), 473, 474; and "Phillis' Reply to the Answer in our last by the Gentleman in the Navy," dated "December 5th, 1774," appeared in the same magazine Jan. 1775, pp. 34, 35. Both of these poems appear in Mason, pp. 81-84; 86-87. Dated "Providence, Oct. 26, 1775," "To His Excellency General Washington," another *Proposal* title was published in *The Pennsylvania Magazine,* April, 1776, p. 193), then edited by Thomas Paine. Widely republished since, it has appeared, e.g., in Charles F. Heartman's *Phillis Wheatley/(Phillis Peters)/Poems and Letters/first collected edition/with an Appreciation by Arthur A. Schomburg* (New York, 1915), and in G. Herbert Renfro, *Life and Works of Phillis Wheatley* (Washington, D.C., 1916). "An Elegy/Sacred to the Memory of . . ./Dr. Samuel Cooper" was part of a pamphlet dated "Boston, Jan. 1784," original with the Massachusetts Historical Society, and was reprinted in Heartman, where also was republished "Liberty and Peace," a pamphlet in the New York Historical Society in 1784. "To Mr. and Mrs.——, on the Death of their infant Son" appeared in *The Boston Magazine in September,* 1784, p. 488, and again in Mason, pp. 95-97. "On the Capture of General Lee," although dated as early as "Boston, Decr. 30, 1776," and included as a *Proposal* title, remained in manuscript for "politically censorious" reasons until the October 1863 publication in the *Proceedings of the Massachusetts Historical Society,* VII (1863-64), 165-67. It has since been republished by Heartman and Renfro.

THE PROSE

Phillis Wheatley's "prose" consists of her correspondence to various persons. It includes 1 letter to the Reverend Samson Occom, Mohegan Indian minister while he was in England during 1765; another from England to Occom in Boston, and a third letter written February 11, 1774, published the next month in several New England newspapers; 1 letter to General George Washington, dated "Oct. 26, 1775"; 3 letters to her benefactress in England, the Countess of Huntingdon, dated "Boston, October 25, 1770"; "London, June 27, 1773"; "London, July 17, 1773"; 7 letters to a fellow Black female domestic living in Newport, Rhode Island (the dates run from May 18, 1772 through May 10, 1779); 1 letter to a certain "L" as a covering letter for an early version of "On Recollection"; 2 letters to the Reverend Samuel Hopkins, abolitionist Congregationalist in Newport. The letters which Phillis wrote to her fellow domestic, Obour (sometimes spelled "Arbour") Tanner in Newport were first published in *The Proceedings for the Massachusetts Historical Society* for November, 1863, Vol. VII, pp. 267-279, and again, separately and privately as *Letters of Phillis Wheatley, The Negro Slave Poet* (Boston, 1864) with a prefatory paragraph by Charles Deane, early Phillis Wheatley researcher. In 1916, the letters appeared again twice, in the already mentioned books by Heartman and Renfro. When Carter G. Woodson reprinted the letters in *The Mind of the Negro as Reflected in Letters Written During the Crisis: 1800-1860* (Washington, D.C., 1926), he also included the first-time publication of one of the two letters Phillis had written to Reverend Samuel Hopkins, the letter dated "Boston, May 6, 1774," from a manuscript located in Boston's Public Library, Chamberlain collection A.6.20. Benjamin Quarles reprinted a copied version of another of her letters to the Reverend Hopkins, this one dated "Boston, Feb. 9, 1774," in his article "A Phillis Wheatley Letter," *The Journal of Negro History,* XXXIV (April, 1949), 462-4.

Of the numbered titles of letters in her *Proposals,* at least 4 have been published: "I: To the Right Hon. Wm.E. of Dartmouth, Sec. of State of N. America," is published in full in Mason, pp. 110-111, from a manuscript in the Massachusetts Historical Society (the handwriting, on four-paged, lined paper, does not much resemble Phillis' earlier or later handwriting, but a note by "C[harles] D[eane]" attests to its authenticity, concluding that "Phillis learned to write a better hand later."); "7: To the Right Hon. Countess of H——" and "12: To the Rt. Hon. Countess of H——" and "13: To the same" are published by Sarah Dunlap Jackson, pp. 212, 214, 215. The letters have been excerpted elsewhere, e.g., Benjamin Brawley, *The Negro in Literature and Art in the United States* (New York, 1918), pp. 17-23, and Vernon Loggins, *The Negro Author* (Port Washington, N.Y., 1959), pp. 17-25.

REPRINTING OF THE 1773 VOLUME

There are almost two dozens of reprintings of the pioneering volume, *Poems/on/Various Subjects,/Religious and Moral,*/by/Phillis Wheatley,/Negro Servant to Mr. John Wheatley,/of Boston, in New England./ London:/ Printed for A. Bell,/Bookseller, Aldgate; and sold by/ Messrs. Cox and Berry, King—/Street, Boston/MDCCLXXIII. Moreover, it was not uncommon for several of these reprintings to boast of being second and third "editions": e.g., *Memoir and Poems/of/Phillis Wheatley, A Native African and a Slave/* . . Second edition,/Boston . . ./1835; *Memoir and Poems/* . . . Third edition./Boston, 1838. Professor Mason cites the publication dates for at least 19 reprintings of her 1773 volume, running from 1786 through 1930. There are still more; and although they claim to be faithful reprintings of the London 1773 edition, which was based on Phillis' manuscripts, several reprintings have marked variations from the first edition. Some of these variations are explainable as modernized spellings and punctuation, and other variations are printers' errors. But still others consist of omissions of entire lines from poems (e.g., line 15 of "To the University of Cambridge" and line 64 of "Thoughts on the Works of Providence" are missing in the 1802 Walpole, N.H., edition; line 17 of "To the University of Cambridge" is missing in the Geo. W. Light, Boston, 1834 edition). Not only does the text vary in successive reprintings, but the "portraits" of Phillis also differ. It seems that there were originally two similar but not identical engravings of Phillis, both of which were, apparently, used for separate runs of the first 1773 London edition. Then there is a lithographed copy of one of these engravings, and it prefaces the 1834 and 1838 Boston editions, and it seems different from another "likeness" found in the second 1838 Boston edition; the 1916 G. Herbert Renfro edition has still another different "likeness," while the 1919 Philadelphia edition has what looks like a wash painting likeness.

BIOGRAPHY AND CRITICISM

Many of the reprintings of Phillis' volume include biographical sketches of Phillis, but almost oll of them reprint verbatim the facts from the memoir first published for the 1834 Boston edition, written by Margaretta Matilda Odell, "a collateral descendant of Mrs. Wheatley, and . . . familiar with the name and fame of Phillis from her childhood." Of the other sketches, perhaps the worthier ones would include the brief "Phillis Wheatley, the Negro Slave Poet," written by Dr. N. B. Shurtleff for the December 21, 1863 issue of the Boston *Daily Advertiser,* since much republished; and Arthur A. Schomburg's "Appreciation," found in Heartman's *Phillis Wheatley/ (Phillis Peters)/Poems and Letters.* It was Schomburg who introduced (p. 10), but did not document the anecdote, since repeated, about Phillis' conversational charms winning over two racially bigoted daughters of a certain Colonel and Mrs. Fitch.

Mentioned by many people internationally, and especially by Black American authors of literary histories or in race books or in anthologies, Phillis received extended critical treatment only in Benjamin Brawley's *The Negro in Literature and Art,* pp. 1032, 160-63; in Brawley's *Early Negro American Literature* (Chapel Hill, 1935), pp. 31-55; and in Vernon Loggins' book, pp. 16-29. Julian D. Mason, pp. xviii—lv, offers generous samplings of various critical insights. M. A. Richmond's *Bid the Vassals Soar* (Washington, D.C., Howard University Press, 1974) is a recent ambitious interpretation of Phillis (and George Moses Horton), that includes ordinary information.

The Author

A native of Newport, Rhode Island, William H. Robinson, Jr., is a veteran of World War II, and a graduate of New York University (B.A., 1951), Boston University (M.A., 1957), and Harvard University (Ph.D., 1964). He has taught Black American Literature at Prairie View College; A & T State University in Greensboro, North Carolina; Howard University, Boston Univeristy, and Harvard University Extension. He has written for educational radio, stage, and television, has published short stories and poems, and is the editor of *Early Black American Poets* (1969), *Early Black American Prose* (1971), and *NOMMO: An Anthology of Modern Black African and Black American Literature* (1972). He is presently professor of English and Director of Black Studies at Rhode Island College, Providence.